"Engaging, thoughtful, and poignant, *A Daybook for Beginning Nurses* is a wonderful way to launch novice nurses on their journey toward professional self-confidence. It's an extraordinary compilation of inspirational wisdom from some of the profession's most highly respected nurse experts. Full of motivational thoughts and insight, this book helps nurses reflect on what's important as they embark on their new career."

Col. John S. Murray, PhD, RN, CPNP, CS, FAAN
President, Federal Nurses Association

"This book is a must-read for new nurses or for nurses re-entering the profession. It celebrates the emergence of nursing as a profession that has recognized the importance of nurturing, valuing, and inspiring its young. The advice is relevant and credible—obviously coming from nurses who have lived the 'new nurse' experience, mentored others through this process, and gained valuable insight along the way. I wish I'd had this book when I was a new nurse!"

Susan Tocco, MSN, RN, CNS, CNRN, CCNS
Neuroscience Clinical Nurse Specialist
Orlando Regional Medical Center

"This book offers you daily guidance and makes it easy for you to keep track of your thoughts and impressions as a new nurse. Donna Wilk Cardillo has inspired many nurses with her wise guidance and advocacy for new graduates. Follow Donna's example: write down your dreams, your goals, and begin recording the many enduring impressions of your nursing journey.

Diane J. Mancino, EdD, RN, CAE
Executive Director
National Student Nurses' Association
Foundation of the National Student Nurses' Association

Books Published by the Honor Society of Nursing, Sigma Theta Tau International

A Daybook for Beginning Nurses, Cardillo, 2009.

Evidence-Based Design for Healthcare Facilities, McCullough, 2009.

Being Present: A Nurse's Resource for End-of-Life Communication, Schaffer and Norlander, 2009.

Why Retire? Career Strategies for Third Age Nurses, Bower and Sadler, 2009.

B Is for Balance: A Nurse's Guide for Enjoying Life at Work and at Home, Weinstein, 2008.

To Comfort Always: A Nurse's Guide to End-of-Life Care, Norlander, 2008.

Ready, Set, Go Lead! A Primer for Emerging Health Care Leaders, Dickenson-Hazard, 2008.

Words of Wisdom From Pivotal Nurse Leaders, Houser and Player, 2008.

Tales From the Pager Chronicles, Rancour, 2008.

The Nurse's Etiquette Advantage, Pagana, 2008.

NURSE: A World of Care, Jaret, 2008. Published by Emory University and distributed by the Honor Society of Nursing, Sigma Theta Tau International.

Nursing Without Borders: Values, Wisdom, Success Markers, Weinstein and Brooks, 2007.

Synergy: The Unique Relationship Between Nurses and Patients, Curley, 2007.

Conversations With Leaders: Frank Talk From Nurses (and Others) on the Front Lines of Leadership, Hansen-Turton, Sherman, and Ferguson, 2007.

Pivotal Moments in Nursing: Leaders Who Changed the Path of a Profession, Houser and Player, 2004 (Volume I) and 2007 (Volume II).

Daily Miracles: Stories and Practices of Humanity and Excellence in Health Care, Briskin and Boller, 2006.

A Daybook for Nurse Leaders and Mentors, Sigma Theta Tau International, 2006.

The HeART of Nursing: Expressions of Creative Art in Nursing, Second Edition, Wendler, 2005.

Making a Difference: Stories from the Point of Care, Volumes I & II, Hudacek, 2005.

A Daybook for Nurses: Making a Difference Each Day, Hudacek, 2004.

For more information and to order these books from the Honor Society of Nursing, Sigma Theta Tau International, visit the honor society's Web site at www.nursingsociety.org/publications, or go to www.nursingknowledge.org/stti/ books, the Web site of Nursing Knowledge International, the honor society's sales and distribution division. Or, call 1.888.NKI.4.YOU (US and Canada) or +1.317.634.8171 (Outside US and Canada).

A DAYBOOK
for Beginning Nurses

Donna Wilk Cardillo, RN, MA

Sigma Theta Tau International
Honor Society of Nursing®

Sigma Theta Tau International

Publisher: Renee Wilmeth
Acquisitions Editor: Cynthia Saver, RN, MS
Project Editor: Carla Hall
Copy Editor: Jane Palmer

Cover Design by: Gary Adair
Interior Design and Page Composition by: Rebecca Harmon

Printed in the United States of America
Printing and Binding by Edwards Brothers, Inc.

Sigma Theta Tau International
550 West North Street
Indianapolis, IN 46202

To order additional books, buy in bulk, or order for corporate use, contact Nursing Knowledge International at 888.NKI.4YOU (888.654.4968/US and Canada) or +1.317.634.8171 (outside US and Canada).

To request a review copy for course adoption, e-mail solutions@nursingknowledge.org, or contact Cindy Jo Everett directly at 888.NKI.4YOU (888.654.4968/US and Canada) or +1.317.917.4983 (outside US and Canada).

To request author information, or for speaker or other media requests, contact Rachael McLaughlin of the Honor Society of Nursing, Sigma Theta Tau International at 888.634.7575 (US and Canada) or +1.317.634.8171 (outside US and Canada).

ISBN-13: 978-1-930538-87-0

Library of Congress Cataloging-in-Publication Data

Cardillo, Donna Wilk.
  A daybook for beginning nurses / Donna Cardillo.
     p. ; cm.
  ISBN 978-1-930538-87-0
1. Nursing. 2. Nurses--Diaries. I. Sigma Theta Tau International.
II. Title.
  [DNLM: 1. Philosophy, Nursing--Personal Narratives. 2.
Meditation--Personal Narratives. WY 86 C267d 2010]
  RT24.C37 2010
    610.73--dc22
                                                        2009029550
Second Printing, 2016

Dedication

To every individual—past, present, and future—who had the courage, compassion, and conviction to choose nursing as a profession and light up the world in the process.

–Donna Wilk Cardillo

Acknowledgements

Thanks to all the amazing individuals who shared their passion, perspective, and wisdom so willingly and joyfully. I'm grateful for your generosity and enthusiasm.

Thanks to Cindy Saver, Renee Wilmeth, and everyone at Sigma Theta Tau International for bringing this wonderful project to me. You were all such a pleasure to work with. Keep doing what you're doing to inspire and support nurses!

Thanks to Diane Mancino for writing the foreword and for ongoing support. You are such a great role model, mentor, and inspiration to students and nurses everywhere.

Thanks to my amazing husband, Joseph, who is such an enormous help, support, and constant source of encouragement and ideas. I'm so blessed to have you in my life.

Thanks to my wonderful family—my parents, Helen and Stanley Wilk; my sister, Barbara Bastian; my brother, Ed Wilk; my wonderful son and daughters, David, Pia, and Justyna Cardillo; my precious grandsons, Joao "Junior" Miguel and Sebastian Alexander; my mother-in-law, Rose; and my brothers-in-law, sisters-in-law, nieces, and nephews: Barry, Nancy, Eugene, Linda, Paul, Pam, Mimi, Anna, Andrew, Matthew, Lily Belle, Max, and Jasper. Thanks for your support, enthusiasm, and interest. You all add so much to my life.

About the Author

Donna Wilk Cardillo, RN, MA, is the career guru for nurses. She travels the world helping nurses be happy in their careers and reach their full potential. She does that as a keynote speaker, workshop leader, author, columnist, and consultant.

Known as *Dear Donna* at the Gannett Healthcare Group, she writes a monthly column for Nursing Spectrum and NurseWeek magazines and a daily online advice column at nurse.com. Cardillo has been the featured health care careers coach for the *Los Angeles Times* and was the Healthcare Careers Expert at Monster.com.

Cardillo is author of *Your 1st Year as a Nurse: Making the Transition From Total Novice to Successful Professional* and *The ULTIMATE Career Guide for Nurses: Practical Advice for Thriving at Every Stage of Your Career.* She has written for *Imprint,* the journal of the National Student Nurses' Association (NSNA), and has served as keynote speaker for NSNA national conferences. She is a frequent guest on radio and TV, including NBC's "TODAY" show. She is also the country's foremost authority on nontraditional career opportunities for nurses and the creator of the Career Alternatives for Nurses® seminars and home study program.

The recipient of numerous awards, Cardillo is most proud to have been designated a Diva in Nursing by the Institute for Nursing in New Jersey for outstanding achievements and excellence in practice. A lifelong resident of New Jersey, Cardillo lives in Sea Girt at the beautiful Jersey Shore with her husband, Joseph.

Table of Contents

Foreword

"A JOURNAL IS ABOUT EXAMINING YOUR LIFE. IT'S A GPS SYSTEM FOR YOUR SPIRIT."

–QUINN MCDONALD

As I reflect on my career, it is the early experiences that I had interacting with patients, families, and colleagues that have made a lasting impact on my life. When I entered nursing, journaling was not the buzzword it is today. Luckily, I began to keep a diary as a teenager. In nursing school and in my early years of practice, I recorded the stories of my most memorable patients in my journals—beautiful, cloth-bound books. I recently came across one such book while packing my belongings to move to a new residence. After reading and pondering the entries I had made as a new rural public health nurse, I gleaned new lessons and insights that I would never have arrived at if I had not written those impressions years before.

My journals are filled with stories, poetry, one-liners, dreams, and aspirations. Many passages are self-examination questions, such as "What would I have done in this situation?" (thinking about a mother who was learning to care for an infant with severe developmental disability) or "What could I have said to ease this person's pain?" (reflecting on a chronically ill elderly gentleman who married a much younger woman to ensure that someone would be there to care for him in his old age—instead, she became ill and needed his care before she passed away in middle age). You, too, will have experiences such as these to record and recall as you advance in your life and career.

One self-reflection passage that I recorded recounted a conversation I had with a colleague in graduate school. My colleague turned to me and, out of the blue, asked, "What kind of a leader do you aspire to be?" Until that moment, I had not even thought of myself as a leader. Today, I ask myself that question almost every day and write down new insights as they emerge.

This book offers you daily guidance and makes it easy for you to keep track of your thoughts and impressions as a new nurse. Donna Wilk Cardillo has inspired many nurses with her wise guidance and advocacy for new graduates. Follow Donna's example: write down your dreams, your goals, and begin recording the many enduring impressions of your nursing journey.

–Diane J. Mancino, EdD, RN, CAE
Executive Director
National Student Nurses' Association
Foundation of the National Student Nurses' Association

Introduction

Welcome to the wonderful world of nursing! I took such joy in compiling this book for you as a way to share the wisdom, passion, insights, and humor from my experiences and those of our nursing colleagues. While gathering quotes and stories from contributors and other sources, I reflected on the essence of nursing and the profound and sacred work that nurses do. It is just one more reminder of why I am so proud to call myself a nurse.

Nursing is the most amazing profession. It will change you for the better as much as it will positively impact the lives of those you care for. It is challenging and rewarding, exhilarating, and at times exhausting. Saving lives and keeping the planet healthy are hard work! You'll need all the support, encouragement, and determination you can muster in your first year as you begin to build a practice that will blossom into a vocation and, eventually, into a legacy of caring.

Consider *A Daybook for Beginning Nurses* a mentor of sorts, one that gently guides you. Use it to record some of your first-year experiences and reflect on the journey you are embarking on. Read it through in one sitting if you wish, but then read it day by day as you go through your first year and beyond. Pick it up whenever you need some encouragement or need to remember what nursing is all about. Let it remind you of all the nurses who have paved the way for you and all those who are there for you every day, everywhere you look.

Think of each daily and monthly message as a marker on the path—illuminating your way—left by those who have gone before you: a thought, inspiration, meditation, or piece of humor to provide focus for your day, bringing you closer, each and every day, to your destination of being a confident, competent nurse. Use the space provided to jot down your thoughts as you go through your day. Take time later, perhaps at the beginning of each new month, to look back on what you've written and reflect on where you were then—professionally and personally—and where you are now. You may surprise yourself with your wisdom as you grow and develop as a nurse.

Listen to the voices and feel the heartbeat of each nurse contributor—their words written with you in mind. Feel their warmth and their support as they reach out to you from these pages, as they whisper in your ear, as their words echo in your head, nudging you down the path you were destined to walk, keeping in mind that it's all about the journey. I wish you Godspeed.

–Donna Wilk Cardillo, RN, MA

REFLECTING BACK AND LOOKING FORWARD

January is a time of planning and looking forward. But it should also be a time of reflecting on our past accomplishments. There is a natural tendency to focus on where we want to be and how far we have to travel to get there. We often forget to look at how far we've already come.

Reflect on goals you previously set for yourself, such as getting accepted into nursing school, finishing the program, and passing your licensure exam. Consider what it took to get where you are now. Celebrate your achievements and recognize the qualities—tenacity, drive, determination, passion—that brought you to this point. Think about how much you have learned and how you have grown personally and professionally.

Now think about how those qualities will apply to your future in nursing, especially to your first year. You will need to employ all of the same strategies and attributes that got you to this point in your career and life.

Take time to write down your accomplishments from the past year and beyond. Include fears you've overcome or minimized, what you've done for the first time, risks you've taken, new knowledge you've acquired, and all the times you've had to step out of your comfort zone. Thinking about them isn't enough—you need to put them on paper or a computer screen so you can see them, read them, and make them concrete. Make a list of your attributes to remind yourself how strong, resourceful, and resilient you are. Review this list often, especially when you are feeling down and wondering if you can carry on.

–Donna Wilk Cardillo, RN

"Courage does not always roar,
sometimes it is the quiet voice
at the end of the day
saying
'I will try again tomorrow.'"
–Maryanne Radanbacher
Verse contributed by Jes Hockman, RN

January

January 1

"Rome wasn't built in a day, and neither was anyone's nursing career. Set specific goals for the new year—things you'd like to achieve, skills you'd like to master, challenges you'd like to face head-on—that will bring you closer to your dreams of being a confident, competent nurse."

—Donna Wilk Cardillo, RN

January 2

"Envision yourself as a seasoned nurse who handles every situation with confidence and ease. Describe in writing what you'll be like as a nurse 5 years from now—what you'll be doing and how much you will have contributed to the world during that time. Be creative! Think it . . . feel it . . . be it!"

—Donna Wilk Cardillo, RN

January 3

"Always ask for help when you don't know how to do something. The great thing is, you only have to ask the question once, because you'll always know the answer to that question afterward."

–Donna Wilk Cardillo, RN

January 4

"As a new grad, I kept a small pocket notebook for quick reference, where I had written all the information pertinent to my new position. As a seasoned RN, I had a clipboard with protocols, meds information, and important phone numbers. My peers made fun of the clipboard, but many of them looked for it when I wasn't working."

–Roseanne Kelly, RN

JANUARY 5

"There is great joy and personal satisfaction in mastering something that once seemed almost impossible to accomplish. You may be tempted to give up, but when you make up your mind to learn a skill and stick with it until you succeed, it's exhilarating."

—Donna Wilk Cardillo, RN

JANUARY 6

"Staying in periodic touch with your former classmates is an important part of transitioning to professional nursing. Share experiences, tips, feelings, and good advice you received. Offer support and encouragement, and take time to laugh often and cry together as needed."

—Donna Wilk Cardillo, RN

JANUARY 7

"Find time in each day, perhaps before going to sleep, to reflect on your day. Ask yourself: 'Whom did I help today? What did I learn? What do I want to accomplish tomorrow?' It's ideal to write these things down. Self-reflection and planning help to keep you in control and moving forward."

—Donna Wilk Cardillo, RN

JANUARY 8

"It can be very humbling to be in a situation where everyone seems
to know more than you do. But everyone in every profession
started out in the same place. That is part of the process of
becoming experienced and competent. Take each day as it comes,
knowing that at the end of each day, you are more experienced
than you were the day before."

–Donna Wilk Cardillo, RN

JANUARY 9

"Get a system. My preceptor in my first job told me this right
away. Have a mental checklist in your head (or on paper if you
need it), and do things the same way every day. Repetition helps
you build a routine. I approached my charts that way—looking
at them from beginning to end and zeroing in on what nurses are
directly responsible for: orders, care plans, and notes. I also do this
in my assessments and reports (I memorized our report sheet)."

–Colleen Berding, RN

January 10

"Keep an index card in your pocket. Write down at least one thing
you want to find out when you get home. For example, you may
write down drug names, procedures, or disease conditions that you
need to review or learn. This will rapidly increase your knowledge
base and support a lifelong habit of learning. This was the best
thing I did in my first year of practice."

–Kathleen D. Pagana, RN

January 11

"Nurses often have difficulty articulating the essence of what they
do. It is so difficult to put into words the often subtle yet profound
way that nurses impact lives. It is something that must be
experienced, mastered, and emblazoned upon the soul to be
truly and deeply understood."

–Donna Wilk Cardillo, RN

January 12

"New graduates as well as seasoned nurses need to try to be friends
with everyone and avoid cliques. We all have different strengths,
abilities, and weaknesses. Nurses usually work as a team—few
do the job alone. We need each other. Getting along well with
everyone will benefit you and patient care."

—Donna Maheady, ARNP

January 13

"Choosing your first nursing job takes some work. Many people
I know never researched the facility, toured the unit, or talked to
their prospective manager. I researched facility Web sites and called
the human resources department to see who took new grads into
NICU. I requested a tour and met the manager and some of the
nurses at my first job, all of whom were very welcoming and an-
swered my questions. That made a real difference to me."

—Jennifer Tucker, RN

January 14

"Nursing is a fun ride but be forewarned: The first 4 months might feel like you've gotten thrown into the deep end with no life pre-server. But every month it got better. Every month I gained control over one more thing."

–Justine Mize, RN

January 15

"My first emotion after graduation was panic! There was so much to get used to regarding the mechanics of nursing: charting, the computer system, etc. I kept telling myself, 'You have been trained.' But I learned that there is a ton of help out there if you look for it."

–Scott Eddy, RN

January 16

"The things that we do create who we become."
–Laura Lagana, RN

January 17

"The door that nobody else will go in at, seems always to swing open widely for me."
–Clara Barton, Civil War nurse and founder of the Red Cross

January 18

"Who are those who suffer? I do not know but they call to me."
–Pablo Neruda, from The Mountain and the River

January 19

"Set your mind to learning. Rather than focusing on the personalities and communication style of those around you, look for every opportunity to learn something new. Whether the 'teacher' is warm and caring or brusque and slightly rude—there is something to be gleaned from every situation, even if it's learning what not to do next time."

–Donna Wilk Cardillo, RN

January 20

"Always you have been told that work is a curse and labour a misfortune. But I say to you that when you work, you fulfill a part of earth's furthest dream, assigned to you when that dream was born."

–Khalil Gibran, from The Prophet

January 21

"Expect success. Go in to situations only expecting the best to happen, and things will generally go your way. If you go in with negative expectations, it is easier to accept defeat and become demoralized. People are more likely to give you what you want, if you expect them to."

–Edward W. Smith

January 22

"Have a simple business card, a calling card of sorts, made for yourself. Use it to exchange professional contact information with other professionals. It facilitates staying in touch and developing ongoing relationships—a must for creating professional networks."

–Donna Wilk Cardillo, RN

January 23

"Too often we underestimate the power of a touch, a smile, a kind word, a listening ear, an honest compliment, or the smallest of caring, all of which have the potential to turn a life around."

—Leo F. Buscaglia

January 24

"Consider how it feels to be the new kid on the block in any situation. Knowing this, go out of your way to welcome and help new employees and students who come to your unit or workplace."

—Donna Wilk Cardillo, RN

JANUARY 25

"If there's something you're afraid to do, such as a procedure
or having an important conversation with someone, look for an
opportunity to do it as soon as possible. Avoidance or delay only
serves to exaggerate the fear and can become a self-imposed
obstacle to your professional growth and development."

—Donna Wilk Cardillo, RN

JANUARY 26

"The reality of working in the hospital is very different from
the student experience. The first months are overwhelming.
But things get better, so hang in there."

*—Contributed by North Shore University Hospital novice nurse night
shift support group*

JANUARY 27

"Have fun at work. Look for the humor in each day. It's especially important to be able to laugh at yourself. Humor heals and lightens the load."

–Donna Wilk Cardillo, RN

JANUARY 28

"It's very empowering to be able to help people. For example, if a kid gets hurt on the basketball court in my community, I'll know what to do."

–Elizabeth Peirano, RN

JANUARY 29

"You must do the thing you think you cannot do."

—Eleanor Roosevelt

JANUARY 30

"Know your resources. You may not know the answer to a question or how to perform a procedure, but a great nurse knows where to find the answers and solutions."

—Lynn Visser, RN

JANUARY 31

"You know you're a nurse if ... you get excited about attending a conference on septic shock and organ failure!"

—Donna Wilk Cardillo, RN

BUILDING CONFIDENCE AND COMPETENCE

Most new nurses experience "reality shock" in their first job. The real world of nursing is very different from how it appeared from a student's vantage point. No longer under the protective wing and watchful eye of their instructor, new nurses often feel overwhelmed, fearful, and unprepared. The pace seems faster, the patients sicker, and the time allotment for everything shorter.

Believe it or not, almost every new graduate feels that way. What you may not realize is that you still have a lot to learn, and you are not expected to know everything. Nursing school was phase one of your education; your first job is phase two. That's why it is so important to find a job that will help you to build a solid foundation in nursing—a job that offers a comprehensive new-graduate orientation program at least 3-6 months long, complete with preceptor. Some facilities even have coordinators who follow new employees for 1 to 2 years after they are hired.

Most experienced nurses agree that it takes a full year after graduation before you start feeling confident and a full 2 years before you feel some level of true competence. That doesn't mean you have to wait 2 years before you feel more comfortable in the profession. It does mean you are learning and growing every day in your new profession, and you have to be patient with the process.

The good news is that, as a new graduate nurse, you are better prepared for the challenges of nursing than you realize. You have learned, practiced, and been tested on all the basics. Now is the time to start building on that foundation and moving forward— one step at a time.

Is it challenging? Of course it is. But nothing worthwhile is ever easy. The path of the healer can be rocky and steep, but the destination is totally worth the journey.

–Donna Wilk Cardillo, RN

"Every journey begins with but a small step, and every day is a chance for a new, small step in the right direction. Just follow your Heart song."
–Mattie J. T. Stepanek

February

FEBRUARY 1

"A nurse who can start an IV on the first try and insert a catheter without difficulty is not necessarily the good nurse. The patients remember your kind words and kind heart—the warm blankets, the cup of coffee, the pillow, the updates, seeing if there is anything you can do for them or their loved ones at the bedside. They need to hear your words and feel your compassion."

—Anna Montejano, RN

FEBRUARY 2

"As a new graduate, it is difficult to envision that someday you'll be the nurse with 5, 10, 15 or 20 years' experience and the "go to" person on your unit. Before you know it, you'll look back and wonder where the time went. Make each moment count."

—Lynn Visser, RN

FEBRUARY 3

"When you feel like quitting, just remember this: You are more
than you ever thought you could be."

–Laura Lagana, RN

FEBRUARY 4

"Visualize success. What you envision in your mind's eye will man-
ifest itself in your life."

–Donna Wilk Cardillo, RN

FEBRUARY 5

"An expert at anything was once a beginner."

–H. Jackson Brown, Jr.

19

FEBRUARY 6

"I will say this for the bedpan: It introduced me to many interesting people whom I would never have met intimately otherwise, and some of them I will never forget."

—Sheila MacKay Russell from The Lamp is Heavy, *1950*

FEBRUARY 7

"I like to hike, get pedicures, and plan trips so I have something to look forward to. This helps me to manage my stress and live a balanced life."

—Elizabeth Peirano, RN

FEBRUARY 8

"I found it very helpful to involve myself in self-education. I attend
conferences on my own, in my specialty, beyond what my employer
pays for. As an adult learner, I'm hooked on education."

–Scott Eddy, RN

FEBRUARY 9

"I keep learning. I read the charts and if something new comes up,
I look it up. I go to conferences and take CEs for things that are
related to my specialty and some that are not exactly related but
have use to me."

–Colleen Berding, RN

February 10

"Don't buy into anyone's negative stereotypes or opinions about nurses. Some people thrive on negativism. Create your own positive reality. You'll be happier and more successful, and you'll positively influence those around you."

—Donna Wilk Cardillo, RN

February 11

"Always dress well at work—whether wearing scrubs, uniform, business suit, or business casual. Develop a professional image to match the professional person you are. Your appearance makes a loud statement about who you are. You have to inspire confidence in others."

—Donna Wilk Cardillo, RN

FEBRUARY 12

"Nursing is a great profession. At first I felt so out of my league and questioned my career choice. But now I don't regret it at all."

—Justine Mize, RN

FEBRUARY 13

"As soon as you trust yourself, you will know how to live."

—Johann Wolfgang von Goethe

FEBRUARY 14

"Never say 'I'm just a nurse' or 'I'm only an RN.' Be proud of your credential and your role. You've earned that right."

—Donna Wilk Cardillo, RN

FEBRUARY 15

"Obstacles are what we see when we take our eye off of our goal. Keep focused on the ultimate outcome you want, and don't focus on those problems that come up. If you start paying too much attention to the problems with what you are trying to accomplish, it can demoralize you and take time away from moving ahead the parts of the project that are working."

–Edward W. Smith

FEBRUARY 16

"Never get defensive when a patient or family member gets angry or impatient. Just being in a health care setting makes most people nervous and anxious; add in the stress of being sick, and short tempers and high anxiety are understandable. A calm, friendly, and compassionate demeanor will help to smooth things out."

–Donna Wilk Cardillo, RN

February 17

"Keep patients and family members informed as much as possible about tests, medications, procedures, and time schedules. This helps folks feel more calm and in control of their circumstances and surroundings."

–Donna Wilk Cardillo, RN

February 18

"Position yourself today for the position you want tomorrow. In other words, choices you make today will impact where you will be tomorrow. Choose wisely."

–Kathleen D. Pagana, RN

February 19

"You know you're a nurse if ... words like sphygmomanometer and pneumostreptococci roll off your tongue with ease."

—Donna Wilk Cardillo, RN

February 20

"Make an effort to learn something personal about the clients you work with—something about their family, their work, their ethnic background. That helps to keep it real for you and for them."

—Donna Wilk Cardillo, RN

February 21

"The only courage that matters is the kind that gets you from one minute to the next."

—Mignon McLaughlin

February 22

"Ask your nursing coworkers what professional associations they belong to. Then ask if you can tag along next time they attend a meeting. You'll get to know that person better, broaden your horizons, and expand your network. Plus, you won't have to walk in alone!"

—Donna Wilk Cardillo, RN

February 23

"Learn to get in touch with silence within yourself and know that everything in this life has a purpose. There are no mistakes, no co-incidences. All events are blessings given to us to learn from."

—Elisabeth Kübler-Ross

February 24

"Familiarize yourself with the history of nursing. Read books about and by nurses, search the Internet, and attend related lectures. It instills a powerful sense of legacy and pride. When you begin to fully understand your roots in nursing, you will feel greater passion and sense of purpose."

–Donna Wilk Cardillo, RN

February 25

"In life you can never be too kind or too fair; everyone you meet is carrying a heavy load. When you go through your day expressing kindness and courtesy to all you meet, you leave behind a feeling of warmth and good cheer, and you help alleviate the burdens everyone is struggling with."

–Brian Tracy

FEBRUARY 26

"Learn to meditate. It can help you find quiet inner space and connect with your spirit. Daily meditation will help to keep you calm, focused, and more in touch with your intuition or inner knowing."

–Donna Wilk Cardillo, RN

FEBRUARY 27

"You can learn new things at any time in your life, if you're willing to be a beginner. If you actually learn to like being a beginner, the whole world opens up to you."

–Barbara Sher

February 28

"We see the patient in a [hospital] bed, or we think we see him. We think he should be profoundly grateful for all that is done for him. But we frequently fail wholly in appreciating how it must feel to some natures to become dependent on the bounty of others; how it must gall and fret a man or woman of independent spirit to be obliged to occupy a [hospital] bed."

–*Charlotte Adams, from* Ethics in Nursing, 5th ed. 1943

February 29
(FOR LEAP OR INTERCALARY YEARS)

"Nursing care comes in many forms. Sometimes it is the ability to make someone feel physically comfortable by various means. Other times, nursing care improves the body's ability to achieve or maintain health. But often it is an uncanny yet well-honed knack to see beyond the obvious and address, in some way, the deeper needs of the human soul."

–*Donna Wilk Cardillo, RN*

Make a Connection With Patients and Families

One of the most important things you can do as a professional nurse is to be "present" in your work by staying focused on and fully aware that you are charged with caring for a fellow human being. That individual has a life and an existence outside of the health care setting. And yet it is so easy to lose that perspective when you get caught up in performing tasks, following a routine, and trying to stick to a schedule. At the end of the day, it is the personal connection—or lack of it—that matters most to the nurse and the patient.

Make the connection by always acknowledging patients and family members—with eye contact, a smile and handshake if appropriate, a light touch, and a greeting or introduction. This applies to everyone, including patients who are elderly or very young, incapacitated in any way, and even comatose. Just because people can't communicate with words doesn't mean that they are not cognizant of their surroundings or of your presence. It is their body, their personal space, and their psyche that you are invading on some level—even if for the good. Respect and honor that. And, remember that family members are an extension of the patient. They need acknowledgement, care, and attention as well.

There is nothing more devastating than feeling invisible or insignificant because you are ignored or treated like a commodity—as if you are being processed through an assembly line. Combine that uncomfortable feeling with being sick, anxious, and fearful, and you will understand why nurses should get into the habit of always making a connection.

–Donna Wilk Cardillo, RN

"When a nurse encounters another
Something happens
What occurs is never a neutral event
A pulse taken
Words exchanged
A touch
A healing moment
Two persons are never the same"
–Barbara M. Dossey, RN, and Cathie E. Guzzetta, RN

March

MARCH 1

"Explore career options within nursing. Talk to nurses who do different things, attend career seminars and career fairs, and read career-related publications. The more you are aware of your options and the full scope of what nurses are doing, the more empowered you will feel and the less anxious you will be about your future."

—Donna Wilk Cardillo, RN

MARCH 2

"My nursing director told me this, and now I tell new nurses: 'Always pay attention if someone tells you something "feels funny" [not humorous but odd], especially a patient or a patient's relative. Ask questions and investigate further. No one is going to fire you if you take vital signs at an off-time because you think something is up. Get further help from your charge nurse, rapid response team, etc."

—Colleen Berding, RN

MARCH 3

"Try to educate yourself on everything. Nursing is a profession where you want to be a 'Jack of all trades' in a way. Take continuing education courses, read journals, and talk to experienced nurses about everything. There is so much to learn."

—Eric Cascio, RN

MARCH 4

"Always introduce yourself to patients and family members by name and credential. Example: 'My name is Eric Borowsky. I'm a registered nurse and will be in charge of your care today.' Don't remain a nameless, generic entity and thereby minimize your role."

—Donna Wilk Cardillo, RN

MARCH 5

"Find a buddy at work—someone you can talk to and let off steam with."

—*Donna Wilk Cardillo, RN*

MARCH 6

"Believe in yourself and persevere. Don't let anyone discourage you."

—*Nancy T. Viola, RN*

MARCH 7

"Talking about frustrations with others who have the same level of experience really helps."

—*Contributed by North Shore University Hospital novice nurse night shift support group*

March 8

"Really get to know your patients, and base your practice on that.
He or she is more than just a person in pajamas under the sheet.
Have a constant feedback loop. Ask them, 'How did you sleep?
Do you have any pain?'"

—Scott Eddy, RN

March 9

"Don't wait until everything is just right. It will never be perfect.
There will always be challenges, obstacles, and less-than-perfect
conditions. So what. Get started now. With each step you take, you
will grow stronger and stronger, more and more skilled, more and
more self-confident, and more and more successful."

—Mark Victor Hansen

March 10

"Your attitude is contagious. This can be good or bad. If your attitude is negative, that negativity will spread to others. On the other hand, if your attitude is positive, that will spread to others as well. If you want to be around people who are positive, start the process and be positive first. Most things that you want will come to you faster in a positive environment, so take the steps needed to create a positive focus, by being positive yourself."

–Edward W. Smith

March 11

"One of the primary reasons that people stay in a job is because they create a sense of community or 'second family' with their coworkers. Build camaraderie at work by participating in social activities when you can—whether at work (celebrations and holiday parties) or outside of work. Get to know people and reveal a little about yourself."

–Donna Wilk Cardillo, RN

MARCH 12

"Read books and articles about success strategies for new graduate nurses. Benefit from the wisdom of those who went before you. You'll also find validation and confirmation of your own experience, which will help to keep things in perspective."

—Donna Wilk Cardillo, RN

MARCH 13

"When things get tough and you're having a bad day at work, take a few moments to step back, refocus, and regroup. Take a few deep breaths, and step outside briefly if you can. Even a short break can help you to regain your equilibrium and get back on track."

—Donna Wilk Cardillo, RN

MARCH 14

"Let go of perfectionism. Do the best you can each day, get help
when you need it, ask questions when you don't know something,
and just keep moving forward."

—Donna Wilk Cardillo, RN

MARCH 15

"Serving on committees in professional associations is a good way
to meet other nurses, learn more about the profession, and get the
word out about nursing."

—Jennifer Tucker, RN

MARCH 16

"Have role models. Look for those nurses who exemplify competence, professionalism, and compassion in everything they do.
Observe them, work with them when you can, talk to them,
and emulate them."

—Donna Wilk Cardillo, RN

MARCH 17

"Be patient with yourself. In the beginning, everything will take
longer because you're still learning how to do things. Eventually
you'll get into a rhythm, and things will come more easily to you."

—Donna Wilk Cardillo, RN

MARCH 18

"Courage is the art of being the only one who knows you're
scared to death."

—Earl Wilson

MARCH 19

"You are your patient's advocate. If something is not right and the doctor will not listen, do not stop. Go to your charge nurse or fellow coworker who is a strong patient advocate. You must do what is best for your patients. They are counting on you."

–Anna Montejano, RN

MARCH 20

"For the first time I knew the emotion-draining, relentless reality of nursing. From a world where there had been layers of seniors and intermediates between me and the patients, I was suddenly plunged into a dim hushed world where there was nothing between me and their most vital need."

–Sheila MacKay Russell from The Lamp is Heavy, *1950*

March 21

"Get the patient and family members involved in the care as much as possible. It empowers them and takes some of the pressure off you. It's a win-win situation."

—Donna Wilk Cardillo, RN

March 22

"You know you're a nurse if ... you have an overwhelming urge to palpate a visible vein in the antecubital space on the arm of someone you just met in a social situation."

—Donna Wilk Cardillo, RN

March 23

"Show sincere appreciation for those who help you, support you, and encourage you. Say thank you and offer sincere compliments when appropriate."

—Donna Wilk Cardillo, RN

MARCH 24

"Anyone can give up—it's the easiest thing in the world to do.
But to hold it together when everyone else would understand
if you fell apart, that's true strength."

—Unknown

MARCH 25

"Stay the course. Nothing significant was ever accomplished easily
or in a short amount of time. Becoming a competent nurse takes
time, perseverance, and persistence."

—Donna Wilk Cardillo, RN

MARCH 26

"Find your soulmate/s who can walk with you and truly bear witness to your ideas, visions, and possibilities—someone who operates from abundance and not scarcity. This person will listen to your ideas without judging. On days when you think you are going crazy, or when you have been hurt by a colleague or are worried, anxious, fearful—or other ways life seems to show up—they are always there and fully present to 'be with' and not try to fix the situation."

–Barbara M. Dossey, RN

MARCH 27

"Twenty years after graduation, I remain committed to my work with the same sense of awe I had when I started; however, now I understand why. The reasons are clearer now. The care I provide my patients and my colleagues makes a difference despite the sometimes-invisible nature of my work—in that sense I am paradoxically a powerful influence."

–Rosemary Field, RN, from the introduction of Tenderly Lift Me, *by Jeanne Bryner, RN*

MARCH 28

"When you look at another nurse, regardless of his or her age, years of experience, ethnicity, or demeanor, remember that you both got into nursing for the same reasons—to make a difference and to help as many other people along the way as possible. Every nurse has that in common, and that is at the core of everything he or she does."

—Donna Wilk Cardillo, RN

MARCH 29

"I believe that when a person becomes a nurse, they sign on for life. It doesn't seem to matter for how long, or in what branch of nursing one works; there is a certain quality—a spirit, a depth of soul—which is unique to the nurse."

—Echo Heron, from Tending Lives

March 30

"A single, caring individual can make a vast difference and have a positive impact on our world. Each of us has a valuable contribution to make by sharing at least one special talent we possess."

—Laura Lagana, RN

March 31

"Always learn from your mistakes and share those mistakes with others. By sharing with your colleagues, you will be the safety net of a patient somewhere out there."

—Lynn Visser, RN

CONFLICT MANAGEMENT

Conflict is part of the human condition and occurs whenever two or more people occupy the same space. It is a natural part of human interaction. While many people think that conflict is a bad thing, it can often lead to creative solutions, a clearer awareness of issues and challenges, and a deeper understanding of self and others. Learning to deal with conflict when it arises results in a strong character, a more satisfying life and career, and a sense of personal empowerment.

When conflict arises at work, and it always will, there is a tendency to either avoid it or get defensive. But neither of these approaches works. Avoidance creates pent-up hostility, fear, and unnecessary anxiety. Some nurses have quit a job to avoid conflict with a manager, preceptor, or other team member. But that will only work until the next conflict arises and, if repeated, will result in an erratic work history and diminished self-esteem.

So what can you do? For starters, always respect yourself, your role, and your opinion. If interpersonal conflict arises, be ready to stand up for yourself when required. Don't get defensive and never engage in name-calling or abusive language. Consider what role, if any, you may have played in the conflict. Talk things out whenever possible, preferably face to face instead of over the phone. Don't use e-mail to try to resolve conflict! Stay calm and even-tempered. Embrace it as a path to personal development and growth.

Sometimes conflict arises when two or more people have differing opinions about something. Great minds regularly have divergent viewpoints where no one is right or wrong. Don't personalize it; stay focused on the issues. Be open to another point of view and listen intently. Learn to discuss and come to consensus. Two heads are always better than one.

–Donna Wilk Cardillo, RN

"Difficulties are meant to rouse, not discourage.
The human spirit is to grow strong by conflict."
–William Ellery Channing

April

APRIL 1

"We all have embarrassing moments as novice nurses when we do something that feels stupid, say something that sounds stupid to our ears, or ask an inane or obvious question. That's just part of the learning experience and will eventually make a hilarious story to tell your nursing colleagues."

—Donna Wilk Cardillo, RN

APRIL 2

"But if I could only tell you what nursing means to me. It's being close to both life and death and sorrow and gladness. It's holding your fingers on the pulse beat of humanity and feeling akin to God. It's when the barriers are down around you and fellowman and you are admitted to his being because he needs you there."

—By Sheila MacKay Russell, from The Lamp is Heavy, *1950*

APRIL 3

"Attend nursing awards ceremonies when you can at your place of
employment or through professional associations, media outlets,
etc. These events are celebrations of nursing meant to spotlight
all that is good and positive about the profession and individual
members. It's a good reminder of why you got into the profession
and what is possible to achieve."

—Donna Wilk Cardillo, RN

APRIL 4

"The U.S. Postal Service has issued numerous commemorative
stamps over the years honoring individual nurses, including Clara
Maass, Dorothea Dix, Mary Breckinridge, Clara Barton, Phoebe
Pember, Harriet Tubman, Sojourner Truth, and Mary Walker. If
you don't know much or anything about these nurses, spend some
time researching them. Their accomplishments and contributions
to nursing and healthcare will blow you away and make you feel
proud to be a nurse."

—Donna Wilk Cardillo, RN

April 5

"Focus on the positive—in yourself, others, and your work—
and that will become your reality."

—Donna Wilk Cardillo, RN

April 6

"Two men look out through the same bars: One sees the mud,
and one the stars."

—Frederick Langbridge

April 7

"Never tell patients that they have to do something. Explain and
tell them the importance of it."

—Anna Montejano, RN

APRIL 8

"I once heard a nurse say, 'Nurses are so passive. They never do anything.' I responded, 'You need to get out more and meet some new people, because the nurses I know are changing the world in both quiet and boisterous ways.'"

—Donna Wilk Cardillo, RN

APRIL 9

"Sometimes you just have to get away. Don't save vacation days— use them! I thought it was frivolous before, but I go treat myself to a pedicure once a month now. I need time for something that is just for me to recharge, so I have something left for my family and my patients."

—Colleen Berding, RN

April 10

"Here's what I love about nursing: Anything can happen and everything does happen. And at the end of the day, you have a real sense
of accomplishment, of having done something worthwhile."

—Eric Cascio, RN

April 11

"Time management is my biggest challenge—bigger than critical
thinking. They don't always teach you that in nursing school.
Learn from experienced nurses how they do it."

—Honey Beddingfield, RN

APRIL 12

"Do things together with other nurses through professional associations or other avenues. Some of us need a little push."

—Justine Mize, RN

APRIL 13

"Do or do not. There is no try."

—Jedi Master Yoda

APRIL 14

"To serve is to rule."

—Lao Tzu

APRIL 15

"Stepping outside of your comfort zone becomes a way of life in nursing. There is always something new to learn, something new to experience, and something new to master."

—Donna Wilk Cardillo, RN

APRIL 16

"I created a sheet to help me stay organized with feeding times, meds, ventilator settings, etc. I use color coding."

—Jennifer Tucker, RN

APRIL 17

"Some people want to quit as soon as something seems hard or they can't do it perfectly right away. But there is arrogance in that thought process—to think that you could become really good at something with minimal effort, time, or experience. Humble yourself to learning and you'll eventually become an expert."

–Donna Wilk Cardillo, RN

APRIL 18

"Change comes slowly. No matter how badly we want it, it takes time to lose weight, or build muscles, or to learn new skills. Understand this, and build the time and frustration this will cause into your thinking. Keep your persistence up by visualizing your goals, using support groups and lots of self-encouragement. Change comes slowly, but the success is long lasting."

–Edward W. Smith.

APRIL 19

"Be kind, for everyone you meet is fighting a hard battle."

—Plato

APRIL 20

"Nursing offers a multitude of unique moments to make a difference in the lives of others, as well as in our own."

—Laura Lagana, RN

APRIL 21

"Invent your world. Surround yourself with people, color, sounds, and work that nourish you."

—SARK

APRIL 22

"Nursing forces me to think about things I would never have
thought much about otherwise. For example, because I work in
oncology, I had to reflect on my own views about death and dying.
Not typically something someone my age would think about,
but it's a good thing."

—Elizabeth Peirano, RN

APRIL 23

"Make it a point to learn about the bigger picture of health care.
Read health care management publications (find them in a col-
lege or hospital library) and ask directors and administrators about
trends and issues. This will help you better understand where
health care and nursing are going."

—Donna Wilk Cardillo, RN

APRIL 24

"Work to develop a rich spiritual life. Read books and take courses
that help you to explore the metaphysical—that which goes beyond
the physical. Get in touch with your true nature. This is a journey
that lasts a lifetime and one that every nurse must embark upon."

–Donna Wilk Cardillo, RN

APRIL 25

"Expose yourself to people who have ideas that are different from
your own. Being open to other viewpoints and ways of doing things
broadens your perspective and makes you a more well-rounded and
well-informed individual."

–Donna Wilk Cardillo, RN

April 26

"Remain curious and develop a genuine interest in others. If someone does something different than you—works in another specialty, a different role, or even a different occupation—ask them about their work: why they chose it, what they do and don't like about it, what's unique or interesting about it. This will open up your world, not to mention your network, in unexpected ways. It may also help you to decide on a future direction for your own career."

—Donna Wilk Cardillo, RN

April 27

"You cannot be in nursing without having some sense of a higher power. Study other religions and reflect on your own religious views. Talk to others about their views. A deeper understanding of various religious beliefs will enhance your nursing practice."

—Donna Wilk Cardillo, RN

April 28

"You know you're a nurse if ... every time you're out to dinner you are saying a silent prayer that you will not have to initiate the Heimlich maneuver—or even worse, CPR—on any other restaurant patrons!"

—Donna Wilk Cardillo, RN

April 29

"The effect you can have on patients and families is priceless. Find your passion and rise to your potential."

—Lynn Visser, RN

April 30

"There is never a reason to be bored in nursing. There are so many different opportunities, even within a particular position and place of employment. If you're bored, it's your own fault."

—Donna Wilk Cardillo, RN

THE VALUE OF NURSING

Nursing is both an art and a science. While many outside the profession do not fully understand or appreciate what we do, nurses have an enormously positive impact on the health, quality of life, and well-being of the planet. That is an awesome role and responsibility!

Much is often made of the caring nature of nurses, with frequent references to a kind word, a gentle touch, or a reassuring smile. And while those gestures convey caring and comfort, that is only part of the science-based, complex, and often life-saving care provided by nurses. Nursing has its own body of research, theory, and practice standards. We operate under our own license and develop multidimensional care plans for clients. Nurses initiate life-saving measures, use critical-thinking skills, teach, counsel, coach, and consult. We are part of the primary health care team and are front-line care providers. Nurses are care managers, health care experts, skilled clinicians, and patient advocates. We are innovators, nurturers, and healers. No wonder nurses are the largest group of health care professionals—there is so much work to do!

Be proud of who you are and what you do. Speak well of the profession and be a role model. Learn to articulate the value of nursing to others in terms that they can understand and relate to. And if you ever doubt for 1 minute that what you are doing is meaningful, significant, or vital to the very existence of the human race, I want you to reread this and reflect on what life in general and health care would be without nurses.

–Donna Wilk Cardillo, RN

"If only you could sense how important you are to the lives of those you meet—how important you can be to people you may never even dream of. There is something of yourself that you leave at every meeting with another person."

–Fred Rogers

May

May 1

"Character cannot be developed in ease and quiet. Only through experiences of trial and suffering can the soul be strengthened, vision cleared, ambition inspired, and success achieved."

—Helen Keller

May 2

"If you respect yourself and believe that you have a purpose in being where you are, doing what you're doing, no one will ever be able to belittle or harass you. They will only look foolish for trying, because clearly they do not respect themselves."

—Donna Wilk Cardillo, RN

May 3

"Prayer is communication with the Divine. It can be whispered or chanted or written or expressed in the work you do. However it is expressed, it is never in vain."

—Donna Wilk Cardillo, RN

May 4

"Even the most experienced nurse started out exactly where you are now. Keep that thought in your head as you gain new insights, knowledge, and confidence with each passing day."

—Donna Wilk Cardillo, RN

MAY 5

"Use positive self-talk every day to combat the negative chatter in your head. Remind yourself that you've already come a long way, have accomplished a great deal, and are a strong and resilient individual capable of great things. How do I know this about you? You're a nurse!"

—Donna Wilk Cardillo, RN

MAY 6

Celebrate National Nurses Week each year from May 6 to May 12. Remind yourself of all the good you and other nurses do."

—Donna Wilk Cardillo, RN

MAY 7

"At the risk of causing the elite of nursing's professional societies and academia to clench and grind their teeth, I also believe that nursing is a calling, in that nurses possess an abundance of compassion—the wisdom born of the heart. Indeed, one of the basic rewards of nursing is the fulfillment which comes from the knowledge that one has made a positive, often profound difference in another's life."

—Echo Heron, from Tending Lives.

MAY 8

"I love being a nurse. I have loved it every single day of the 30-plus years I have been in it, but not because the work was always easy or because I always felt appreciated or recognized for my efforts. Rather, I love it because I have always known, in a very deep and fundamental way, that I am contributing to the greater good—that I am doing my part."

—Donna Wilk Cardillo, RN

MAY 9

"Hold your head up high each day and march toward your goal."
–Donna Wilk Cardillo, RN

MAY 10

"You have to trust yourself and your abilities."
–Jennifer Tucker, RN

MAY 11

"As a man in nursing, my friends rib me about [my career choice].
But don't let it get to you. Nursing is a very respectable profession
with so many opportunities."
–Eric Cascio, RN

MAY 12

"Happy birthday, Florence Nightingale! Read books by and about
Flo. It's amazing how so much of what she wrote so many years ago
still holds true."

–Donna Wilk Cardillo, RN

MAY 13

"As nursing continues to evolve and the scope of practice widens,
it is important to respect and honor those from our past who have
been instrumental in shaping the nursing profession, and our
world."

–Laura Lagana, RN

MAY 14

"To be an effective healer, you must work on your own healing every day. That involves tending to your physical, emotional, and spiritual health and healing. You must practice what you preach."

–Donna Wilk Cardillo, RN

MAY 15

"No one is perfect or knows everything—not even the most experienced practitioner. Perfection is not the goal in nursing. The goal and the commitment are to continually move forward by expanding your knowledge and experience base."

–Donna Wilk Cardillo, RN

May 16

"The harder I work the more I live"
—*George Bernard Shaw*

May 17

"You know you're a nurse if ... you are always scouting out where
the nearest AED (Automatic Electronic Defibrillator) is in a public
place, just in case you need to use it."
—*Donna Wilk Cardillo, RN*

May 18

"Treat yourself well. You deserve it."
—*Donna Wilk Cardillo, RN*

MAY 19

"The moment you think you're 'too old' to learn something new, you begin to decline. Age is a state of mind, and learning new things helps to keep you young and engaged in life. That's the secret to eternal youth—never stop learning, at any age."

—Donna Wilk Cardillo, RN

MAY 20

"Volunteer to be on a committee at work related to something you're interested in or want to learn more about. It exposes you to new people and new information, and you never know where it will lead."

—Donna Wilk Cardillo, RN

May 21

"Nursing is not for everyone. It takes a very strong, intelligent, and compassionate person to take on the ills of the world with passion and purpose, and work to maintain the health and well-being of the planet. No wonder we're exhausted at the end of the day!"

–Donna Wilk Cardillo, RN

May 22

"I have learned more from talking with others in informal conversation than I ever learned in the classroom. Formal education is of great value, but some of the most practical and interesting information I have acquired comes from those I encounter in my daily life—when I stop to listen."

–Donna Wilk Cardillo, RN

MAY 23

"Don't take rejection personally. Everyone encounters rejection, every day. But not everyone handles it well. Some people quit, some people cut back, but others press on. Be the one who presses on."

—Edward W. Smith

MAY 24

"I never stop asking myself questions all day, such as 'Why am I giving this medication? Why is this patient still in the hospital?' If they're still here because of nausea and vomiting, I ask myself, 'What can I do to alleviate that?' This all helps me in my assessments."

—Elizabeth Peirano, RN

May 25

"Regardless of your situation, face each day with hope and
optimism. Only the hopeful believe that change is possible—
either in yourself or in those around you."

–*Donna Wilk Cardillo, RN*

May 26

"If you love your work, that will come through in everything you
do. It will inspire confidence and trust in those you care for and
will uplift those you work with."

–*Donna Wilk Cardillo, RN*

May 27

"Start a journal. You think you will remember experiences early in
your career, but before you know it, time will pass as if it was the
speed of light. Having a collection of past experiences to look back
on will touch you as a nurse."

–*Lynn Visser, RN*

May 28

"There is a tendency with some people, that when they become enlightened through education and experience, they feel the need to leave those who are less enlightened behind. In truth, the truly enlightened soul shines that light on those around them until those lights shine as bright."

—Donna Wilk Cardillo, RN

May 29

"A nurse can make the difference between a positive and a negative health care experience. Even if the patient has a negative experience with another practitioner or some aspect of care, the nurse has the opportunity, the ability, and the responsibility to put things in perspective for that patient and make things right."

—Donna Wilk Cardillo, RN

May 30

"Find an avenue to talk about your day, either to family members, friends, or coworkers. Don't keep things bottled up inside. When you share things with another, you lighten your load and gain a broader perspective."

—Donna Wilk Cardillo, RN

May 31

"It's impossible to know how many lives you've touched, saved, or improved in nursing. But you will always know that the world is a better place for your having been in it."

—Donna Wilk Cardillo, RN

SELF-CARE

Nurses are caregivers by profession and by nature. That means that we are always looking out for the welfare of others. Unfortunately, in the process, we often overlook self-care. Because we work in a high stress profession, that tendency can have devastating personal and professional consequences.

When you expend a lot of energy—whether physical, emotional, or spiritual—it is absolutely essential that you take steps to replenish that energy on a regular basis. While self-care is perceived by some as selfish or "a luxury," for nurses it is vital to our very survival and well-being as humans and as professionals.

A stressed, depleted nurse makes more errors, has less energy and stamina, has poor judgment, is impatient and less focused, and is on the road to burnout—the dreaded condition that occurs when a person's energy output chronically exceeds intake and replacement. Nursing is stressful by its very nature; thus, making self-care a priority is your professional responsibility. Honor and nurture yourself and your work by getting into a regular habit of energy renewal and stress management. Take care of your physical, emotional, and spiritual health. Find ways to disengage from your work in your daily routine, as well as during extended periods of time off, such as vacations.

The life force has a natural rhythm of intake and output. Just as the sun rises and sets, the ocean ebbs and flows, we breathe in and out, we sleep and wake up—so too must you create a system of regular energy renewal to balance energy expenditure. It must become the rhythm of your existence to create balance, harmony, health, and well-being.

–Donna Wilk Cardillo, RN

"In dealing with those who are undergoing great suffering, if you feel 'burnout' setting in, if you feel demoralized and exhausted, it is best, for the sake of everyone, to withdraw and restore yourself. The point is to have a long-term perspective."

–14th Dalai Lama, Tenzin Gyatso

June

JUNE 1

"Surround yourself with positive, motivated, upbeat people. Seek
them out in your life at work, through professional associations,
and in your community. You adopt the attitudes and outlook of
those you spend your time with."

—Donna Wilk Cardillo, RN

JUNE 2

"A lot of nursing is logistics—you need the right people and stuff
in the right place at the right time. Some is trial and error, but you
can reduce the error if you ask others how they do it. Some nurses
are happy to tell you; others may not be. Your nonlicensed staff
may have tips for you too, so watch them."

—Colleen Berding, RN

June 3

"Do something fun on your day off."
—*Donna Maheady, APRN*

June 4

"Nursing is the hardest job you'll ever love."
—*Donna Wilk Cardillo, RN*

June 5

"Keep things in perspective. You might think you know how to do something, but watch, learn, and listen."
—*Scott Eddy, RN*

June 6

"Learn the art of patience. Apply discipline to your thoughts when you become anxious over the outcome of a goal. Impatience breeds anxiety, fear, discouragement, and failure. Patience creates confidence, decisiveness, and a rational outlook, which eventually lead to success."

—Brian Adams

June 7

"All nurses start out thinking that they'll never learn everything they need to know to be a great nurse. The exhilaration comes when you finally realize that you can be a great nurse at every stage of the learning curve. It's not all about what you know."

—Donna Wilk Cardillo, RN

JUNE 8

"Be a positive role model, even as a new nurse. Be respectful, friendly, and professional to everyone. Stay even-tempered and nonreactive to emotional outbursts."

—Donna Wilk Cardillo, RN

JUNE 9

"You shouldn't avoid new experiences. You should welcome them. In not accepting them when they're offered to you, you restrict your own thought and capabilities. You lose a part of yourself."

—Sheila MacKay Harvey, from The Lamp is Heavy, *1950*

JUNE 10

"Nursing may be your life's work, but it's not your whole life.
Spend equal time on your family, yourself, and outside interests
for balance."

—Donna Wilk Cardillo, RN

JUNE 11

"Florence Nightingale's lamp is an appropriate symbol for nursing,
because in a figurative sense, nurses bring light into dark places."

—Donna Wilk Cardillo, RN

JUNE 12

"Tradition guides, but experience teaches."

—Adam Frank, as quoted in Tricycle Magazine

June 13

"Every day, ask yourself, 'How can I be a better _____?' Whatever
you want to be better at should be reviewed every day. Remind
yourself every day that you want to get better at something you are
working on, and make it a point to think about it. This will bring
gradual progress in key areas of your life, and after a period of
time, you will be a true expert in something you care about."

–Edward W. Smith

June 14

"For me, nursing transcends the notion of a job; it transcends the
notion of a career. For me, nursing is bigger than that—it is a
lifestyle. As nurses we have the opportunity to extend our caring
practice not only to our patients but also to our colleagues, friends,
loved ones, families, community, nation, and potentially the world.
We can touch their lives and hearts and make a difference
in so many ways."

–Valentina Gokenbach, RN

JUNE 15

"In nursing school, it's always go, go, go. You think you have to
keep that up after you graduate, but you don't. You're learning
so much in the beginning—your brain is on overload.
You have to rest."

–Jennifer Tucker, RN

JUNE 16

"The best way to get ancillary staff to help is to approach the work
as a team and say, "Let's go in and assist the patient together."

*–Contributed by North Shore University Hospital novice
nurse night shift support group*

June 17

"Don't burn your bridges. Keep past relationships with professors, veteran nurses, former coworkers, and preceptors. You never know who you'll run into in the future and who may be your future manager!"

—Eric Cascio, RN

June 18

"The vast majority of nurses love what they do—that's always the way it's been. You can align yourself with the positive majority or the negative minority. The choice is yours."

—Donna Wilk Cardillo, RN

June 19

"A life is not important except in the impact it has on others' lives."
—Jackie Robinson

June 20

"Nurses are not invincible. To be successful, they need to take care of themselves first."
—Laura Lagana, RN

June 21

"Always thank your nurse, sometimes the only one between you and a hearse."
—Carrie Latet

June 22

"In any hospital and most places of employment, you have access to a wide range of experts—social workers, therapists, case managers, pharmacists. Tap into their specialized knowledge and experience whenever you can. Most folks love to teach and appreciate being consulted."

—Donna Wilk Cardillo, RN

June 23

"Keep a log of positive things that people—coworkers, patients, family members—say about you, including any nice notes you receive. Review it often, especially when you're having a bad day, to remind you why you do what you do and to keep propelling yourself forward."

—Donna Wilk Cardillo, RN

JUNE 24

"Regardless of your age or past experience, you are the future of nursing. You are not bound by old stereotypes or traditions. You have an opportunity to create a new paradigm. You will create the future direction of the profession."

—Donna Wilk Cardillo, RN

JUNE 25

"Come to work with an upbeat attitude. It will rub off on everyone you encounter throughout the day and will not only make your day better, but theirs as well."

—Jenny Herrick, RN

JUNE 26

"You know you're a nurse if ... you think nothing of eating salad or popcorn out of an emesis basin (a clean one, of course) with a tongue blade as a spoon."

–Donna Wilk Cardillo, RN

JUNE 27

"Sometimes getting the cup of water for a patient or family member makes all the difference. Although other daily duties may be more important to you, the simple things often mean the most to them."

–Lynn Visser, RN

June 28

"Whether a person is a male or female, a nurse is a nurse."

–Gary Veale

June 29

"I always tell my preceptees, 'I don't necessarily care if you know exactly what is wrong with the patient, as long as you know there is a problem and you get help.'"

–Elizabeth Peirano, RN

June 30

"Be a fierce patient advocate at all times. That patient and their family are depending on you to look out for their best interests, even if it means questioning other health care providers."

–Donna Wilk Cardillo, RN

EFFECTIVE COMMUNICATION

Communication is the foundation of all success and is vital in nursing. One of the biggest challenges you will face is the need to continually modify your language use when you communicate with people of diverse backgrounds, such as physicians, managers, patients, or coworkers. By remembering some basics, you'll always do well.

Be mindful of using clear, simple language when speaking to patients and family members. Don't use jargon and acronyms. (This is not always easy for us to do!) Some acronyms apply only to your specialty; even a nurse or other health care professional from another specialty may not be familiar with the terminology. If you speak in a way that the other person doesn't understand, you may as well have remained silent.

Some nurses have lost the ability to speak in a manner that others can understand. They have become fluent in "nurse-speak," a combination of regular English mixed with medical and nursing terminology, and sometimes forget whom they're talking to or how they're saying what they're saying. Phrases such as "Activities of Daily Living" or "ADLs" become part of our standard vocabulary, but mean nothing to people who don't work in the industry. Instead, use clear, descriptive language such as "bathing, grooming, and eating." Break it down into simple language and you'll never go wrong.

Learn to listen well. Sometimes an angry or frustrated person—whether coworker, patient, or family member—needs to be heard first and foremost. Many difficult situations can be diffused, not to mention better understood, just by attentive, mindful listening.

All of this gets easier with practice and eventually will become natural if you consider to whom you are speaking, make a concerted effort to choose your words carefully, and listen attentively.

–Donna Wilk Cardillo, RN

"Communication leads to community, that is, to
understanding, intimacy, and mutual valuing."
–Rollo May

July

July 1

"Nurture yourself and your coworkers. If you notice someone is having a bad day, ask if you can relieve them for a few minutes or if there is anything you can do to help them. Sometimes just making the gesture is all that is needed to lift their spirits."

–Donna Wilk Cardillo, RN

July 2

"You don't have to be confident to act confident. Stand tall with your head upright, look people in the eyes, and speak in a clear, audible voice. Act like you have a right to be there, even if you don't feel that way. Sometimes you have to fake it 'till you make it."

–Donna Wilk Cardillo, RN

JULY 3

"When someone offers you a compliment, whether a patient, family member, or coworker, graciously accept, even if you don't feel worthy. By so doing, you honor yourself and the person who gave you the compliment."

–Donna Wilk Cardillo, RN

JULY 4

"Once you enter the profession, you will never be the same. Your life will be inextricably changed. You will develop an appreciation for life and a respect for death, beyond that of the average person. You will see the best and worst of the human spirit, and you will become a better, more passionate person because of this."

–Donna Wilk Cardillo, RN, from Your 1st Year as a Nurse: Making the Transition from Total Novice to Successful Professional

JULY 5

"At an appropriate time, ask seasoned nurses to tell you about when they were new graduate nurses—what their biggest challenges were and how they overcame them. It might help them to better relate to you and your challenges, and you may get some good advice!"

–Donna Wilk Cardillo, RN

JULY 6

"One of the surprises that I experienced as a new [RN] graduate was the fact that I had to direct LPNs who were far more experienced than I. They'd seen it all and knew it all and were waiting for me to expose my ignorance. I learned to ask them their opinions and respect their knowledge."

–Pat Iyer, RN

July 7

"Once a nurse, always a nurse. No matter where you go or what you do, you can never truly get out of nursing. It's like the Mafia. You know too much!"

—Deb Gaudlin, RN

July 8

"I have developed outside hobbies. I write more than I used to, and that keeps me sane."

—Colleen Berding, RN

July 9

"Experience: that most brutal of teachers. But you learn, my God do you learn."

—C.S. Lewis

July 10

"Consider creating a scrapbook about your first year in nursing and beyond. Include photos, poems, inspirational quotes, notes from patients, an occasional written update or journal excerpt by you, etc. It will be good to look back on as you move along in your career, and eventually you may want to share it with future and prospective nurses!"

—Donna Wilk Cardillo, RN

July 11

"Be kind to someone, and you will get an increase in energy. Do a favor for someone, and you will feel better right away. Doing something nice or helping someone in some way makes us feel better, so if you want to feel better, one way is to do something nice for someone else."

—Edward W. Smith

July 12

"In Bill Murray's 1991 movie 'What About Bob?', Bill plays a loveable neurotic named Bob to Richard Dreyfuss' uptight psychiatrist character, who wrote a book titled *Baby Steps*. Whenever Bob would get nervous or scared, he'd repeat to himself, 'Baby steps, baby steps,' to remind himself to just put one foot in front of the other and move forward. Try 'channeling' Bob the next time you're feeling anxious and overwhelmed. The technique works for me and always puts a smile on my face when I think of 'Bob' saying it."

—Donna Wilk Cardillo, RN

July 13

"When you're trying to make a decision—whether it's about accepting a job offer, going back to school, or making a job change—after you've gathered the appropriate background information and talked it over with loved ones, a good rule of thumb is to follow your heart and go with your gut. That will always lead you in the right direction."

—Donna Wilk Cardillo, RN

JULY 14

"Always ask for help when you need it. Some people won't offer it
unless asked. Better to ask, even at the risk of feeling inept, then
not asking and potentially causing harm to a patient."

—Donna Wilk Cardillo, RN

JULY 15

"I believe that everyone who comes into our lives is sent to teach us
something. And sometimes the most difficult people are the ones
we learn the most from."

—Donna Wilk Cardillo, RN

JULY 16

"Every workplace includes people from a variety of age groups,
backgrounds, ethnicities, and levels of experience. You can focus
on your differences, or you can look for the commonalities
and celebrate both."

—Donna Wilk Cardillo, RN

JULY 17

"Contrary to what you might have heard, the vast majority of nurses are friendly, caring individuals who are more than happy to help and support you in your new career. If you don't experience that in your workplace, you may need to look for a new job or ask to transfer to another department."

—Donna Wilk Cardillo, RN

JULY 18

"You can't just assess a patient at 8 a.m. and be done with it. I am assessing all day long—checking the IV rate, heart rate, color, change in condition. You have to be vigilant."

—Elizabeth Peirano, RN

July 19

"You can't live a perfect day without doing something for someone who will never be able to repay you."

–John Wooden

July 20

"If your nursing school has an alumni association, join it. Your nursing program was a big part of your life, and it's a great way to stay connected."

–Donna Wilk Cardillo, RN

July 21

"You can do what you have to do, and sometimes you can do it even better than you think you can."

–Jimmy Carter, former U.S. president

July 22

"If you doubt you can accomplish something, then you can't accomplish it. You have to have confidence in your ability, and then be tough enough to follow through."

—Rosalynn Smith Carter, former U.S. first lady

July 23

"One of my nursing professors told me, 'Don't do anything just for the money. You can get lured by big sign-on bonuses, etc. But you have to enjoy what you're doing, no matter what it is."

—Eric Cascio, RN

July 24

"Start making plans to attend a state or national nursing convention. It is exhilarating and empowering to meet nurses from across the country and realize that you are part of a greater whole."

—Donna Wilk Cardillo, RN

July 25

"Set professional goals each year and post them where you will see them every day. Always be striving for something. When you reach your goal, set one that is more challenging. This will keep you moving in a positive, forward motion in your career."

–Donna Wilk Cardillo, RN

July 26

"Find an online community of nurses that you like—there are quite a few of them. It's a great place to go after a long day to vent, get support and advice, or share a good cyber-laugh."

–Donna Wilk Cardillo, RN

JULY 27

"Don't get hung up on 'finding your niche' in nursing. Most of us have had different niches at different times in our careers. Sometimes you have to try on different hats before you find one that fits—until your hat size changes."

–Donna Wilk Cardillo, RN

JULY 28

"I always volunteered for things at work that my coworkers didn't want to do, such as teaching in the community, working on a research project, or creating the monthly schedule. I didn't do it to impress anyone, but rather because I wanted to challenge myself and learn new things. That always kept it fresh and interesting for me. After 30 years in nursing, I'm still learning and trying new things all the time."

–Donna Wilk Cardillo, RN

July 29

"If you have special abilities such as technology skills, volunteer for a related project at work. It's a good way to showcase your talent, and it makes you more visible."

—Donna Wilk Cardillo, RN

July 30

"Obtain your national certification in your area of focus."

—Lynn Visser, RN

July 31

"You know you're a nurse if ... you never get a cold or a bladder infection again, only a URI or a UTI."

—Donna Wilk Cardillo, RN

THE COMMUNITY OF NURSING

When you enter the nursing profession, you become part of a global community—one that exists beyond your place of employment, beyond your state of residence, and even beyond your specialty. How exciting is that?

As such, you have an opportunity as well as a responsibility to become an active member of that community. You do this by getting active and participating in nursing professional associations; by staying in touch with nursing colleagues who you meet through various modes of communication and community; and by attending nursing conferences, conventions, and even career fairs.

I sometimes hear new graduates say, "Oh, I don't have time to go to meetings and conferences." We all find time for those things that are important to us. And often you don't realize the benefits until you're actually engaged in a community. Or perhaps you're thinking, "I need to focus on getting more experience first—I can get involved in outside activities later." The truth of the matter is that you need that larger community of nursing more than ever when first getting started in the profession. If you don't connect, you're missing out on so much.

Immerse yourself in the community of nursing. Make a commitment to be a contributing member and take advantage of all that the profession has to offer.

–Donna Wilk Cardillo, RN

"In our hectic ... fast-paced society, it's common to feel
overwhelmed, isolated, and alone. Many are rediscovering
the healing and empowering role that community can bring
to our lives. The sense of belonging we feel when we
make the time to take an active role in our [professional]
communities can give us a deeper sense of meaning
and purpose."

–Robert Alan

August

August 1

"The differences between nursing and many other occupations are significant. You can't be scared. You have to jump in with two feet. It's not a job you do halfway. You have to totally immerse yourself in it."

—*Tom Alicandri, RN*

August 2

"Read the book *You Can Heal Your Life*, by Louise Hay. You can also find the movie version on DVD. The book is about how your thoughts govern your life and health. It has implications for you in your own life and for the patients you work with."

—*Donna Wilk Cardillo, RN*

AUGUST 3

"Be flexible with career options. There are so many fields within
nursing, so stay open to them."

–Eric Cascio, RN

AUGUST 4

"Use your defeats to grow. Every time you suffer a setback, analyze
what went wrong and learn from it."

–Edward W. Smith

AUGUST 5

"Don't criticize, complain, or gossip at work, unless you want to be
the recipient of same."

–Donna Wilk Cardillo, RN

August 6

"Our appearance is a powerful communication tool, sending messages to every sighted person. Everyone is highly influenced by the visual impression of a person they are meeting for the first time."

—Catherine Bell

August 7

"Use daily affirmations. Repeat: 'I am a valuable member of the team. My contributions make a positive difference. I have a right to be treated with respect.' Say anything often enough, and you'll start to believe it."

—Donna Wilk Cardillo, RN

August 8

"There was a time that I was convinced I had no ability to write, yet today I am a nursing author and columnist. Stretch yourself to find out what you are capable of. Sometimes you just have to try things, even at the risk of looking like a fool."

—Donna Wilk Cardillo, RN

August 9

"I sometimes hear nurses say, 'I don't belong to my professional association because my employer doesn't reimburse me for it.' If you're leaving your professional development up to your employer, you'll be in a sorry state. Take personal responsibility for your own career and be proactive with it."

—Donna Wilk Cardillo, RN

AUGUST 10

"It never hurts to say a little prayer to yourself as you're heading to your workplace that 'this is going to be a goooood day ... because I'm going to make it that way ... with your help!'"

–Jenny Herrick, RN

AUGUST 11

"Something about nurses, they never rest.

When you see one coming toward you, you are being head-to-toe assessed!

It may look as if they are passing you by, but instead they've made a note.

Skin turgor, scleral color—and that's just above the throat!"

–Song lyric from "Nurses Never Rest," by Deb Gaudlin, RN

AUGUST 12

"I pray a lot and have an inner trust that God's going to take care of my day. I trust that he'll take care of those things that are out of my control."

—Honey Beddingfield, RN

AUGUST 13

"Nurses are vital at the bedside, but we are just as vital in every other area of health care. Don't be afraid to look beyond the traditional role."

—Donna Wilk Cardillo, RN

AUGUST 14

"Don't ever underestimate the amount of intelligence, science, and skill needed to be a great nurse. We make it look easy because we're so good at what we do."

Donna Wilk Cardillo, RN, from "I Save Lives. You?"

August 15

"A little humility and an eagerness to learn go a long way."
—Nancy T. Viola, RN

August 16

"Healing yourself is connected to healing others."
—Yoko Ono

August 17

"They want to have a fabulous listener; they want sweet tenderness
and no sense that you are in a hurry."
—Patch Adams

AUGUST 18

"Learn everything you can, anytime you can, from anyone you can—there will always come a time when you will be grateful you did."

–Sarah Caldwell

AUGUST 19

"Think creatively. Many a nurse has devised a new and innovative way of doing something. Some even hold patents for their inventions on teaching tools, equipment, etc."

–Donna Wilk Cardillo, RN

AUGUST 20

"If a patient is cold, if a patient is feverish, if a patient is faint, if
he is sick after taking food, if he has a bed-sore, it is generally the
fault, not of the disease, but of the nursing."

–Florence Nightingale, from Notes on Nursing, *1881*

AUGUST 21

"The aspect of nursing that amazes me every time I go to work is
the concept of intimacy with my patients and their families.
I am not considered an outsider or stranger to them. I am their
confidant and caregiver. Being with a family in a time of crisis,
illness, or grief is a true privilege that most will never experience
in their line of work."

–Jennifer Eagle Payan, RN

August 22

"Sometimes it is the smallest act of kindness or attention that
means the most to people."

—Donna Wilk Cardillo, RN

August 23

"For everything there is a season ... a time to be born and a time to
die."

—Ecclesiastes 3:1-2

August 24

"They don't care how much you know until they know how much
you care."

—Common advice given to new graduates

August 25

"I held her hand, looked her in the eye, and told her the procedure
was all over. Then I said, 'I was there the whole time.' Little did
I know those words would be like magic to this mother who had
just lost her daughter. As an organ transplant nurse, I was one
of the last people to touch this 17-year-old when her heart stopped
beating. She generously gave the gift of life to seven people by
donating her organs. I gave the gifts of compassion and respect
to the mother and the patient. When the mother called me
her 'angel' for watching over her daughter, I knew I had received
the greatest gift a nurse could be given."

–Lynn Visser, RN

August 26

"Your time is limited, so don't waste it living someone else's life.
Don't be trapped by dogma—which is living with the results of other
people's thinking. Don't let the noise of others' opinions drown out
your own inner voice. And most important, have the courage to follow your heart and intuition. They somehow already know what you
truly want to become. Everything else is secondary."

–Steve Jobs

August 27

"To be an advocate for a person at a vulnerable time in life is an honor. When a patient calls you an angel for the first time or the 15th time, you will know you are doing what you were meant to do."

—Lynn Visser, RN

August 28

"Step outside during your workday, even for a few movements, when you can. The change of scenery and fresh air, the feel of sunshine on your face, and the sights and sounds of the outdoors can reenergize and revitalize you."

—Donna Wilk Cardillo, RN

August 29

"Sometimes family members want to help with the care of
their loved one. Let them; it makes them feel good that
they are helping."

—Anna Montejano, RN

August 30

"Perfection does not exist. Do your absolute best and, when
uncertainty creeps in, consult with others. We learn from
each other. Your turn to be the teacher will come."

—Laura Lagana, RN

August 31

"Nurses are the heart of health care."

—Donna Wilk Cardillo, RN

Lifelong Learning

Your basic nursing education is complete—yeah! But your education is hardly over. In fact, now that you are a licensed nurse, you must make a commitment to lifelong learning.

Information and skills rapidly change in nursing and health care. You need to tap into a pipeline of continuous information to keep up on industry standards and trends. You have an obligation to your license, yourself, and your patients to stay abreast of the most current information, research, and practice standards related to your specialty and nursing in general. That responsibility does not fall entirely on the shoulders of your employer. Rather, it is your professional duty.

So how can you do all that? Immerse yourself in learning through reading and research, and by attending seminars and classes on an ongoing basis. Discuss and debate nursing and health care issues and trends with colleagues to get different perspectives. One of the best ways to stay current is by joining and becoming active in your professional nursing associations. Through the related publications and by attending meetings and educational programs, you can stay on top of issues and information. Work on professional development skills such as writing, public speaking, effective communication, and more. Do it on your own time and on your own dime if necessary.

Make plans to continue your formal education. Education is a gift that you give yourself and is an investment in your future, regardless of how long you plan to stay in the workforce. Higher education will enrich your life in ways you can't imagine. It broadens your perspective on the world; helps you get to know yourself and your profession better, regardless of your major; and makes you a more well-rounded individual. Well-rounded people are happier, more competent, and more confident.

–*Donna Wilk Cardillo, RN*

"Education is light; lack of it, darkness."
–*Russian proverb*

September

SEPTEMBER 1

"Find a mentor early in your career. Not only will the mentor enhance your career, but you will better theirs."

–Lynn Visser, RN

SEPTEMBER 2

"You know you're an ED or Ortho nurse if ... you are tempted to adjust the arm sling of a perfect stranger that you pass in the mall."

–Donna Wilk Cardillo, RN

SEPTEMBER 3

"The most important practical lesson that can be given to nurses is to teach them what to observe."

–Florence Nightingale

September 4

"Find a way to deal with stress. I didn't always deal with it well in the beginning, but it builds up if you don't find an outlet. Talking, exercise, music, and vacations, even day trips, help. I now talk more to my wife about my work."

—Eric Cascio, RN

September 5

"After working years in critical care, I've come to realize that what is a priority to me in caring for my patient is completely different from what is important to the family. Before visiting hours, I will have taken the patient to CT scan, changed the chest tube dressings, and resolved some oxygenation issues. I will have eight drips hanging, three of which I'm titrating, and be infusing blood. But when that family walks in the room, the first thing they will notice is that I washed and combed their loved one's hair—they will be confident that they are getting the best nursing care ever."

—Jennifer Eagle Payan, RN

September 6

"The simple act of caring is heroic."
–Edward Albert

September 7

"Getting on committees at work helps you to get known."
–Jennifer Tucker, RN

September 8

"The combination of caring and competence is what good nursing
is all about."
–Donna Wilk Cardillo, RN

September 9

"Learn some simple yoga or stretching movements that you can do anywhere, any time during your workday. Stretching helps to keep you physically and mentally alert and focused, keeps your body more flexible, and can serve as brief respite from your day."

—Donna Wilk Cardillo, RN

September 10

"While humor is not appropriate in every case, using humor with patients and family members, once trust has been established, can be very therapeutic for the caregiver and care recipient. It has been shown to reduce pain, reduce blood pressure, decrease stress hormones, and neutralize tense situations. Learn to use it well."

—Donna Wilk Cardillo, RN

September 11

"I don't know anyone who enjoys going to the hospital. To help remedy this, I got an idea to create a Laugh Room in the pediatric ward of hospitals."

–Joseph Barbera, of Hanna-Barbera cartoon fame

September 12

"Start and end each day with gratitude. Be thankful for your current level of health—even if it isn't perfect—for the opportunity to live and give another day, and to be able to say, 'I made a difference today.'"

–Donna Wilk Cardillo, RN

September 13

"Remember, you're there for the patients, and they come first no matter what. You wouldn't have a job if it weren't for them (nor would the doctors!)"

—Jenny Herrick, RN

September 14

"They said, 'You can't work as a psych nurse right out of school. You'll forget your skills!' I worked as a psych nurse anyway, because I was drawn to it. I later transitioned into the ED. Boy, did that psych experience come in handy."

—Donna Wilk Cardillo, RN

September 15

"You've got to get up every morning with determination if you're
going to go to bed with satisfaction."

—George Lorimer

September 16

"Commit random acts of kindness at work without expecting
anything in return. You reap what you sow."

—Donna Wilk Cardillo, RN

SEPTEMBER 17

"The more you challenge yourself—the more you educate yourself—and the more you master new skills, the more you will learn about yourself and your capabilities. Getting to know yourself in the above ways is the path to self-actualization."

–Donna Wilk Cardillo, RN

SEPTEMBER 18

"Spend some time in the public library when you can. The stacks are filled with books, magazines, DVDs, and CDs that are educational, motivational, and inspirational. The library is a spiritual place for personal growth and development."

–Donna Wilk Cardillo, RN

SEPTEMBER 19

"A smile is the light in your window that tells others that there is a caring, sharing person inside."

—Denis Waitley

SEPTEMBER 20

"Laugh at yourself before others have a chance to."

—Donna Wilk Cardillo, RN

SEPTEMBER 21

"There's an intimate relation between caring and curing."

—Ashley Montagu

September 22

"Don't let someone else tell you what your nursing career should or shouldn't be. Every nurse is different, so follow your heart and carve out your own niche in nursing."

–Donna Wilk Cardillo, RN

September 23

"Treat every member of the health care team as you wish to be treated—with respect, patience, and compassion. What goes around comes around."

–Donna Wilk Cardillo, RN

September 24

"Learn from your mistakes; don't dwell on them. You can't undo the past, no matter how deep the regrets. Move on to a better life, knowing more for the future."

—Joseph Cardillo

September 25

"There are only two ways to live your life. One is as though nothing is a miracle. The other is as though everything is a miracle."

—Albert Einstein

SEPTEMBER 26

"Treat everyone with the same respect and care. Whether someone is a VIP or a drug abuser, they should both be treated with respect. There are times when a nurse may be disrespectful to a patient addicted to drugs. We are not here to judge—we know nothing about their life, how it started out, what they have been through. Comfort them and be kind."

–Anna Montejano, RN

SEPTEMBER 27

"Treat every day like a special day. Each day is in fact special, even though we may not think it is. Every day gives us a new chance to work on our goals, a new chance to enjoy the progress we have made, a chance to work, and a chance to play."

–Edward W. Smith

SEPTEMBER 28

"Continued patience, persistence, and perseverance eventually
produce success."

–Laura Lagana, RN

SEPTEMBER 29

"You are the most important person in your life."

–Julie Fuimano, RN

SEPTEMBER 30

"The patient was trembling as she told me she was 20 weeks pregnant and her water had broken while flying across the country. She was 3,000 miles from home, scared, and alone. I assured her she was at one of the best obstetric and neonatal facilities in the country. She lost the baby that day but later told me, 'You are doing what you are meant to do with your life.' Often, compassion and sharing your heart are just what a patient needs. Never be afraid to share your heart with your patients. You may be the only person they have at that moment in time."

–Lynn Visser, RN

CAREER MANAGEMENT

Your career in nursing is just starting—congratulations! While much of your energy and focus will initially be on getting acclimated to the profession and your new workplace, you need to start creating a plan for your future.

Career management is your roadmap to success. It is a systematic process of keeping your career on track and moving forward in a positive direction. It involves setting long- and short-term goals and updating them as you reach them. It requires the creation of an action plan to achieve those goals. It encompasses developing a network of peers and others to support you along the way, continuously exploring career options, and accumulating experiences. Its purpose is to enhance your current and future career opportunities.

Read career books and attend nursing career seminars. Whether happily employed or not, get out regularly to career fairs to assess the current job market and learn about opportunities. Stay visible in your profession and develop professional relationships both inside and outside of your place of employment, and even outside of nursing. Use volunteering, professional association involvement, and your job to develop new skills, showcase your special talents, boost your credibility, and refine those skills you wish to further develop such as leadership, writing, teaching, project development, and research.

–Donna Wilk Cardillo, RN

"Think not of yourself as the architect of your career but as the sculptor. Expect to have to do a lot of hammering and chiseling and scraping and polishing."

–B.C. Forbes

October

October 1

"I went into nursing to help others. What I found that was interesting was how the patients had helped me too. Life doesn't go one way—sometimes we help others and sometimes others help us."

–Lynn Durham, RN

October 2

"I once heard someone say that nurses are 'bedside leaders.' I love that because we really are! We're the ones who get to know the patient and the family. We're the communication link between the patient and the doctor."

–Elizabeth Peirano, RN

OCTOBER 3

"To unwind, I like to watch movies and comedies and get lost in them. It's a good diversion."

–Eric Cascio, RN

OCTOBER 4

"Unless someone like you cares a whole lot, nothing is going to get better. It's not."

–Dr. Seuss, from The Lorax

OCTOBER 5

"To love what you do and feel that it matters—how could anything be more fun?"

–Katherine Graham

OCTOBER 6

"Nurses have consistently been ranked number one in Gallup's annual list of occupations rated for honesty and ethical standards. (The exception is 2001 after the 9/11 tragedy, when firefighters temporarily moved into that slot.)"

–Donna Wilk Cardillo, RN

OCTOBER 7

"When confident, nurses are open to other perspectives, listen respectfully, and are able to advocate for themselves and patients!"

–Beth Boynton, RN, from e-newsletter Confident Voices for Nurses

October 8

"Expand your view of who a nurse is and what a nurse does. Don't get locked into a narrow view of a nurse's role. There are many ways and places to make a difference, both direct and indirect, and innovative nurses are finding new ones all the time."

–*Donna Wilk Cardillo, RN*

October 9

"I considered dropping out of nursing school during my last semester because I thought I just didn't know enough and didn't have what it takes. We can be so short-sighted with ourselves. Today I bask in the warmth of experience, thankful that I took a chance on myself."

–*Donna Wilk Cardillo, RN*

136

OCTOBER 10

"Once you become a nurse, you have an image and reputation to uphold. Everything you do, both in and out of work, will reflect on the profession as a whole. Take that responsibility seriously."

–Donna Wilk Cardillo, RN

OCTOBER 11

"As you move forward in your nursing career and gain knowledge and experience, always look for ways to help and support those who follow you. Teaching is a great way to keep learning."

–Donna Wilk Cardillo, RN

OCTOBER 12

"Create a vision of the kind of nurse you want to be. Then do whatever it takes to mold yourself into that ideal. Be relentless in pursuing that goal and celebrate the journey."

–*Donna Wilk Cardillo, RN*

OCTOBER 13

"A nurse is a nurse is a nurse—whether providing patient care at the bedside, teaching in an academic setting, or being at the helm of a nursing publication. Healing and health promotion take place on many different levels in many different ways.

–*Donna Wilk Cardillo, RN*

OCTOBER 14

"The best way to get something done is to begin."

—Anonymous

OCTOBER 15

"You know you're a nurse if ... you have a plastic airway in your home first aid kit and a Kelly clamp in your kitchen drawer."

—Donna Wilk Cardillo, RN

OCTOBER 16

"Find the friendly, competent people in your workplace and align yourself with them."

—Donna Wilk Cardillo, RN

OCTOBER 17

"Taking care of the bodies of the sick is sacred. Someday you will
be the patient. Be the nurse you want to see above your bed."

—Jeanne Bryner, RN

OCTOBER 18

"Don't be nervous about being nervous. There is a fine line between being too nervous and not nervous enough. Some nervous-
ness can give you the focus and energy you need to be your best,
too much puts you in the panic zone, and too little puts you to
sleep. Act your way into the way you want to be. If you want to be
more nervous, act more nervous; if you want to be less nervous, act
less nervous and your body will take you where you want to be."

—Edward W. Smith

OCTOBER 19

"Sometimes we are so busy taking care of other people that we don't take such good care of ourselves. To be strong enough to give compassionate, competent care, we need to nurture ourselves physically, mentally, and spiritually every day, even if it is only for 15-minute increments to eat, rest, breathe, laugh, play, or pray."

–LeAnn Thieman, LPN

OCTOBER 20

"Don't be afraid to ask for help. Don't let the fear of what others will think of you, of being vulnerable, or of being wrong keep you from seeking out the assistance you need. We all need help from time to time. And we all make mistakes; it's how we learn, grow, and become better."

–Julie Fuimano, RN

OCTOBER 21

"In times of difficulty we must not lose sight of our achievements, must see the bright future, and must pluck up our courage."

—Mao Tse Tung

OCTOBER 22

"Don't forget that not only do patients need you, but their visitors and loved ones do too. Oftentimes they get left out when it comes to a little TLC."

—Jenny Herrick, RN

OCTOBER 23

"There may be times in your career when you realize you spend all day caring for others, and you feel no one is caring for you. Always remember to nurture yourself or seek out someone who will nurture you. You will care for your patients and their families better if your personal fuel tank is full."

—Lynn Visser, RN

OCTOBER 24

"In spite of all the changes in health care today, nursing still offers rich and diverse opportunities. For those willing to leave old stereotypes behind, to step outside of their comfort zone, and to avail themselves of all that this glorious profession has to offer, the challenges, rewards, and means for self-actualization and fulfillment are great."

—Donna Wilk Cardillo, RN, from The ULTIMATE Career Guide for Nurses: Practical Advice for Thriving at Every Stage of Your Career

October 25

"Start by doing what is necessary, then what is possible, and suddenly you are doing the impossible."

—St. Francis of Assisi

October 26

"Nurses are the real heroes of health care."

—David Letterman

October 27

"A good nurse is a nurse to others. A great nurse is a nurse to herself first, then others."

—Kathy Dempsey, RN

OCTOBER 28

"You never know when you will be the answer to someone else's prayers."

–Barbara Bartlein, RN

OCTOBER 29

"Stay in touch with your instructors after graduation from your nursing program. They are always there for you and can be a great source of support, inspiration, and information."

–Donna Wilk Cardillo, RN

October 30

"Find the inner strength to keep moving forward even when you want to give up. Too many people give up just as they're on the verge of making a breakthrough. You can do anything that you set your mind to, if you want to do it badly enough and are willing to put in the time and the work."

–Donna Wilk Cardillo, RN

October 31

"While getting ready to transfer an extremely unstable patient from ED to ICU, I put a family off many times. 'Just have them wait; they can see him up in the unit.' After he coded in the elevator and died in the ICU, his family still sat in the waiting room. I had gained nothing in my 'busy' time, but the family had lost everything. The times that you are too busy with an unstable patient to have family come in are the times when it is essential to have them at the bedside. Not only will they see your efforts, but it may be their last moments with them."

–Jennifer Eagle Payan, RN

Becoming Part of the Team

When you're the new kid on the block in a new job, you need to take steps to get to know the people, procedures, routine, policies, and politics of your new workplace. Instead of waiting for others to approach you, go out of your way to introduce yourself to physicians, staff members from all shifts, and people from other departments whom you encounter. The more people you know and who know you, the easier and more enjoyable your work will be.

Show a genuine interest in your new coworkers by asking them what they do, how long they've been there, and what they did before. Ask them what one thing you need to know to make their job easier. Read job descriptions, so you are clear on what everyone's responsibility is and can delegate appropriately or ask the right person for help when you need it. Do a lot of listening, observing, and learning in the beginning. Don't be too quick to interject your ideas and viewpoints about the way things are done. Give everyone a chance to get to know you, and you them, and learn to work within the rhythm and routine of your new workplace. Look for opportunities to take a meal or coffee break with various members of the team—not just the nurses. Participate in social activities such as holiday parties, occasionally going out together after work, and potluck suppers.

Even if you're shy and uncomfortable in social situations, force yourself to do this to show you are a member of the team. Isolation can sometimes be misinterpreted as snobbery. Contrary to the old adage, familiarity often breeds respect. Don't wait for someone to offer to help you. Look for ways to help others right from the start. Of course, getting your own work done is a priority, but offer to help turn a patient, get someone out of bed, run for some supplies in a pinch, etc. If you take the lead, others will return the favor.

–Donna Wilk Cardillo, RN

"The nice thing about teamwork is that you always have others on your side."
–Margaret Carty

November

November 1

"Don't be afraid to give your best to what seemingly are small jobs. Every time you conquer one, it makes you that much stronger. If you do the little jobs well, the big ones tend to take care of themselves."

–Dale Carnegie

November 2

"Look for opportunities to try your hand at something new at work, such as presenting an in-service or attending a career fair with the recruiter. Accumulate experiences. This is a good way to discover what you're good at and what you enjoy doing. You'll be building an impressive résumé, and you never know when you might want or need that skill or knowledge."

–Donna Wilk Cardillo, RN

November 3

"When individuals come together and connect with their hearts, we will be in awe of the beauty we find there, and we will see we are more alike than different. As we consciously celebrate the unique gifts and patterns and colors each person brings, we will discover that we are one grand, harmonious design, a community of richness and strength."

—Lynn Durham, RN

November 4

"Some days you will feel you learned a ton in nursing school, and other days you will feel you have a serious knowledge deficit and wonder what you are doing caring for such a complex patient. Always remember you are not alone in these emotions. Every nurse has been there at some point in his or her career."

—Lynn Visser, RN

November 5

"Grow through an experience, rather than just go through the experience. Everything that you are exposed to, good or bad, is an experience. And experience can be a great teacher."

–Edward W. Smith

November 6

"It's important to know your resources. You have online resources for drug and diagnostic information, but you also have senior nurses, pharmacists, dietitians, the chaplain, etc. It's not just you! Use the interdisciplinary team."

–Elizabeth Peirano, RN

November 7

"The only work that will ultimately bring any good to any of us is
the work of contributing to the healing of the world."

–Marianne Williamson

November 8

"Persistence and determination will always win out in the end!"

–Donna Wilk Cardillo, RN

November 9

"If you're not enjoying your job ... you're wasting your life!"

–Jenny Herrick, RN

NOVEMBER 10

"Ask experienced nurses about when and why they got into nursing. Everyone likes to talk about themselves and tell their story. It helps to keep things light."

—Donna Wilk Cardillo, RN

NOVEMBER 11

"No one accomplishes anything significant alone. Build a success team by surrounding yourself with mentors, advisors, experienced nurses, and other supporters. Allow them to help you and provide feedback, encouragement, and advice."

—Donna Wilk Cardillo, RN

November 12

"Remember to share good stories! Don't just recall the hard ones—
repeat the fun, uplifting, touching ones that remind us why we
entered this great profession ... and why we stay."

—LeAnn Thieman, LPN

November 13

"You know you're a nurse if ... you triage the laundry when at
home: This pile needs immediate attention; this pile can wait; this
pile, with a little stain stick, will be OK until you get back to it."

—Donna Wilk Cardillo, RN

November 14

"Don't live your nursing career (or your life) under the radar screen. There is still that old culture that nurses do their job out of the goodness of their heart and neither thanks, appreciation, or acknowledgement is necessary. Get over it and boldly claim what is yours!"

–Joan Borgatti, RN

November 15

"As a new graduate, anything you are unsure of, uncomfortable with, and afraid to do should be faced head-on and done as often as possible while you have your preceptor to guide you."

–Tracey Wolfman, RN

NOVEMBER 16

"Learn everything you can. Ask questions. Soak up knowledge like a sponge and make regular deposits into your bank of information. Some day, when you need to make an urgent withdrawal, you'll be glad you were so eager to learn."

–Laura Lagana, RN

NOVEMBER 17

"There are qualities that make a nurse a great nurse. Define those qualities or attributes for yourself; then decide which qualities you want to espouse and practice living those qualities. Whatever you do as you navigate through life, developing the characteristics that are important for you will help you become not only a better nurse, but a better person too."

–Julie Fuimano, RN

November 18

"When you work hard, you have to play hard. Fun, diversionary downtime is vital for health and harmony in your life."
—Donna Wilk Cardillo, RN

November 19

"Look for the small miracles in your day, and you'll find them everywhere."
—Donna Wilk Cardillo, RN

November 20

"Far and away the best prize that life has to offer is the chance to work hard at work worth doing."
—Theodore Roosevelt

NOVEMBER 21

"How you feel about your profession has everything to do with the value you place on the work you do. If you understand the impact and importance of what all nurses do, you will never question your career choice. Make it your business to understand what nursing is all about."

—Donna Wilk Cardillo, RN

NOVEMBER 22

"You can't copy somebody else and their habits. Everyone has bad habits. You have to take a little something from everybody you work with and find your own zone."

—Eric Cascio, RN

November 23

"Never underestimate the importance of your work, the power of
your knowledge, and your ability to touch the lives of your clients
and their families."

—Susan Scanland, GNP-BC

November 24

"Never bend your head. Always hold it high.
Look the world straight in the face."

—Helen Keller

November 25

"Don't stay isolated in nursing—that is a sure way to fail. Stay connected to former classmates, get active in professional associations, and become part of the team at work."

−Donna Wilk Cardillo, RN

November 26

"Keep in mind that nurses and physicians are partners in health care—both have the same goals and mission. You're both part of the primary health care team and work in tandem with one another, each with a different role. One is not more important than the other, so don't be intimidated by them."

−Donna Wilk Cardillo, RN

November 27

"There were many times in my career when I had to say to someone more experienced than I, whether a physician, nurse, or nurse's aide, 'I haven't done this before. You'll have to show me what to do.' It was never easy to say but always opened up the door to learning."

—Donna Wilk Cardillo, RN

November 28

"Remember to listen to your geriatric patients; they can give you more than you could ever give them!"

—Tracey Wolfman, RN

November 29

"Some of the worst people or events you are exposed to can be good learning experiences for you. Don't shut off learning, just because you are not happy, or even if you are very happy. Learn from everything, both the good and the bad."

—Edward W. Smith

November 30

"Nurses have a tremendous potential to optimize health care systems! With almost 3 million of us, we are health care's biggest workforce and are visible in just about any health care setting. By our very presence, we impact the culture of our workplaces. When we are thriving, we navigate incredible stress while providing highly skilled, compassionate, and rewarding service. The interconnectedness of quality, safety, creativity, and morale is enhanced beyond measure."

—Beth Boynton, RN, from the introduction to Confident Voices

LEADERSHIP

Every nurse is a leader from day one. You lead the health care team, manage patient care, and facilitate positive outcomes. You don't need to have the title "charge nurse" or "nurse manager" to do those things. You are a leader right where you stand.

Leadership is a set of skills and principles—an attribute—rather than a specific job title. Leaders are role models and an inspiration to those around them. They are good communicators and enthusiastic members of the team. Leaders respect themselves as well as other members of the team. They are the epitome of professionalism and excellence in everything they do, regardless of their level of experience or education.

Leaders don't tell others what to do, but rather inspire others to do their best. You have a greater ability to influence your surroundings than you may realize. Work to cultivate your leadership capabilities. Always be aware of the great responsibility you have in the role of health care leader. Do your part to have a positive impact—and lead.

> "A leader is someone who has a sense of what is right
> and has that at the heart of everything they do."
> –Donna Wilk Cardillo, RN

December

December 1

"Show interest. No one ever gets in trouble by showing too much interest, too much enthusiasm, etc., for the things they are involved in. People like you to show interest in what they are interested in, so if you want them to be interested in you, you have to be interested in what they are interested in."

–Edward W. Smith

December 2

"Instead of pointing fingers at the health care industry for not recognizing nursing (the 364 days that don't fall on Nurses Day), ask yourself what kind of person you have to be to change that mindset."

–Joan Borgatti, RN

DECEMBER 3

"If you fear your greatness, you limit yourself. When you limit yourself, you are left with a sense that you could do so much more. The world loses out because you are not giving all that you have— to BEING YOU! The more 'you' you are, the greater the impact you have on the world."

–Julie Fuimano, RN

DECEMBER 4

"In nursing, you're helping your patients physically and emotionally. Sometimes the emotional part can be the toughest. I took a job working for an organ donation organization. The emotional part of the position was too much for me, and I had to switch jobs. But that's OK—I learned something about myself in the process."

–Eric Cascio, RN

DECEMBER 5

"Every time you step out of your comfort zone, you become a little braver, a little wiser, and a little better equipped to face the world."
—Donna Wilk Cardillo, RN

DECEMBER 6

"Always do the right thing. Shortcuts always fail when it comes to nursing!"
—Tracey Wolfman, RN

DECEMBER 7

"You can observe a lot just by watching."
—Yogi Berra

DECEMBER 8

"I love all the opportunities in nursing. I know I can work in the inpatient or outpatient setting, with adults or children. I can teach or do a lot of other things. Nursing is really flexible. I don't feel trapped and I could never be bored."

–Elizabeth Peirano, RN

DECEMBER 9

"As long as you have enough anxiety to keep you humble, and enough humility to keep you from being overly confident or arrogant, you will achieve stability and success."

–Laura Lagana, RN

December 10

"Create a 'book of brains' that you carry with you. Include helpful hints and low frequency procedures in it. Being prepared as an RN includes knowing where your resources are."

–Lynn Visser, RN

December 11

"We learn by example and by direct experience, because there are real limits to the adequacy of verbal instruction."

–Malcolm Gladwell, from Blink: The Power of Thinking Without Thinking, *2005*

December 12

"Live and work with passion, and never, never, NEVER
give up on your dream!"

—Marti Hand, RN

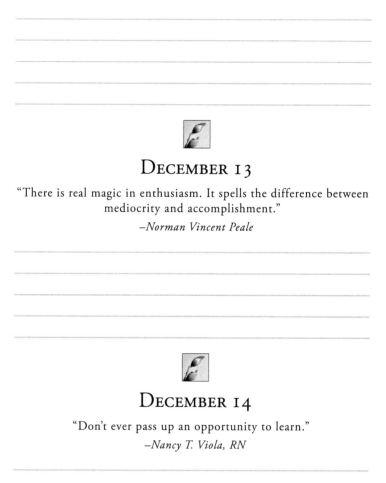

December 13

"There is real magic in enthusiasm. It spells the difference between
mediocrity and accomplishment."

—Norman Vincent Peale

December 14

"Don't ever pass up an opportunity to learn."

—Nancy T. Viola, RN

December 15

"Nursing will take you anywhere you want to go. Nurses work with computers, on cruise ships, in the aerospace industry, in their own businesses, at the helm of hospitals and government agencies, on the battlefield, and at the bedside. I don't know of any profession that is more diverse."

—Donna Wilk Cardillo, RN

December 16

"The nursing profession has been one of the great loves of my life. I love our history; I love all the opportunities that I have had and will have in the future; and I love to think about all the ways that past, present, and future nurses have or will make a difference. I am so proud to be a nurse."

—Donna Wilk Cardillo, RN

December 17

"How wonderful it is that nobody need wait a single moment before starting to improve the world."

—Anne Frank

December 18

"Promise me you'll always remember: You're braver than you believe, and stronger than you seem, and smarter than you think."

—Christopher Robin to Pooh

December 19

"Do the best you can each day, and vow to do a little better the next."

—Donna Wilk Cardillo, RN

DECEMBER 20

"Our workplaces can and should be positive, supporting environments where we practice our profession in an atmosphere of respect. As more and more of us set limits and insist on appropriate behavior, we will automatically become proactive partners in establishing reasonable workloads, cost-effective quality, safer care, and healthy work-life balances."

—Beth Boynton, RN, from Confident Voices

DECEMBER 21

"This is the true joy in life—being used for a purpose recognized by yourself as a mighty one; being thoroughly worn out before you are thrown on the scrap heap; being a force of nature instead of a feverish, selfish little clod of ailments and grievances, complaining that the world will not devote itself to making you happy."

—George Bernard Shaw

DECEMBER 22

"Now that you are a member of this honorable profession of caring, invite others to join. Remind them of the joy, the privilege of touching a life and making a difference. Together, we as nurses can end our own shortage if we 'each one reach one' nurse!"

—LeAnn Thieman, LPN

DECEMBER 23

"Be patient with yourself and the process of learning. Some things can't be rushed. Each day that you 'practice' nursing, you will be one step closer to being the kind of nurse you long to be."

—Donna Wilk Cardillo, RN

December 24

"Move forward in faith, and the right path will eventually
reveal itself to you."

—Donna Wilk Cardillo, RN

December 25

"A single conversation with a wise man is better than 10 years
of study."

—Chinese proverb

December 26

"Anyone who stops learning is old, whether at 20 or 80."

—Henry Ford

DECEMBER 27

"Lighten up. Life should be fun. Many of us forget that there is more to life than work and worry. Remember that deep down, the whole purpose of everything you are doing is to make yourself and/ or others happy."

—Edward W. Smith

DECEMBER 28

"Take a step back and ask yourself if you have put some fun in your plans. Don't postpone enjoying yourself too long. Keep a balance in your life, and remember that fun is a legitimate goal. You will work better because of it."

—Edward W. Smith

December 29

"All meaningful change starts from within. Firm up the boundaries in your personal and professional life. It's impossible to be disrespectful to anyone who possesses a strong sense of self and firm boundaries."

—Joan Borgatti, RN

December 30

"When I think about all the patients and their loved ones whom I have worked with over the years, I know most of them don't remember me, nor I them. But I do know that I gave a little piece of myself to each of them and they to me, and those threads make up the beautiful tapestry in my mind that is my career in nursing."

—Donna Wilk Cardillo, RN

DECEMBER 31

"You know you're a nurse if ... all the love, admiration, and gratitude of the thousands of lives you have touched in every aspect of
your life and work over the years is why you keep on doing what
you do, for all of your days."

—Donna Wilk Cardillo, RN

NOTES

NOTES

NOTES

NOTES

Author Index